£2-99

Haunted Worces

by

Anne Bradford

Haunted Worcestershire

by

Anne Bradford

Foreword by Barrie Roberts

Hunt End Books

Hunt End Books

66 Enfield Road, Hunt End, Redditch,
Worcestershire, B97 5NH, England
Telephone: 01527 542516

First published December 1996
ISBN 0-9519481-1-3

Photographs by Anne Bradford
Design by Edwin Bradford

Made and printed in Great Britain by
BPC Wheatons Ltd, Hennock Road,
Marsh Barton, Exeter, Devon EX2 8RP

Front cover: *Old fishponds, Bordesley Abbey Meadows.*

Acknowledgements

Worcestershire librarians, especially Philip Davis of Redditch Library; Rodney Cole, for his 'voice of reason'; Hilda Wilkes and Betty Cooper of the Bordesley Society; Ian Hayes; Ann Jones. Also: Kidderminster Shuttle, Evesham Admag, Alcester Chronicle, Bromsgrove Messenger, Stourbridge News and BBC Radio West Midlands.

Editors or publishers of the following have allowed stories originally written for (or by) them to be used: John Roberts, Publisher; Jill Manley of BBC Hereford & Worcester Radio; Worcester Evening News, Redditch Advertiser, Berrows Worcester Journal, Redditch Standard.

CONTENTS

WORCESTERSHIRE HILLS (139)

FOREWORD

by Barrie Roberts

Worcestershire lies in the heart of the most haunted area in the world - the British Isles. It would be surprising if it could not produce as good a crop of ghosts and paranormal events as any county in England, and this book proves that it can.

The proof that ghosts exist lies in the many and varied stories herein. If ghosts do not exist, then the people of Worcestershire who supplied these stories must be hysterical, deluded or fraudulent and, of course, the vast majority of them are not. They may not be able to explain what they saw or heard or felt, but they know that it was something. They also know that it was something out of the ordinary. All over Worcestershire - all over Britain - ordinary people experience ghosts every day.

What they experience, as this book shows, can be very varied. We use the word 'ghosts' to label a variety of things, which probably originate from different sources. The sudden appearance of an old friend or relative at the moment of their death is very common. It seems entirely reasonable that, in the last moments, the human mind should reach out to loved ones and contact them telepathically, and since telepathy has been proved over and over again in the laboratory you have a simple, logical explanation of deathbed apparitions, but the same explanation will not cover other phenomena.

Some of the cases in the book are of poltergeists - a German word which means 'noisy ghost'. The phenomenon occurs in every land and is documented back to the beginning of history, but even our forefathers, who believed that ghosts were the spirits of the dead, began to realise that poltergeists were something different. Late in the 12th century someone told Giraldus Cambrensis of two apparent poltergeists in South Wales. His record of the story formed the earliest British poltergeist report we have. Even eight centuries ago Giraldus, a senior priest, realised that there was something different about the case.

Later researchers seized on the same difference and began to realise that poltergeist manifestations almost always centre around a disturbed youngster, usually but not always a girl. From that observation came the view that some paranormal effects are generated within us.

More than twenty years ago, in Canada, Persinger and Lafreniere approached the question differently and their researches established that quite low intensity electrical disturbances of the frontal lobes of the brain can produce vivid and realistic hallucinations – in other words, some 'ghosts' were produced in us by external influences.

Nevertheless, these researches have only touched the edge of the subject. There are many forms of 'ghost' for which only tentative and unproven explanations exist, and some that have none. Why are ghosts often experienced in buildings that have been disturbed by alterations? Why are ghosts associated with burial places? Why are some ghosts seen, others heard, others again smelt? Why are some ghosts seemingly solid and some transparent? Why can some ghosts touch you and others not?

There are many, many questions to be answered before we begin to understand the subject. When we do, we shall probably find that there are many, many different mechanisms by which ghosts impinge upon our consciousness and when we do, I suspect we shall be able to add a few new 'rules' to our science books.

Before we reach that point we will need certain things. We shall need scientists unafraid to embrace the paranormal in their researches; we shall need enquiring laymen to encourage the scientists; above all we shall need the best evidence for researchers to work on. Therein lies the value of a collection such as Anne Bradford's book. Read it by all means for the pleasurable thrill of a shiver down the spine as you sit by the fire, but consider also that many of the people who supplied the stories are ordinary people telling about something extraordinary that happened to them. That is the proof that ghosts have some kind of reality and, of course, if they happen to other people, they might happen to you, mightn't they? Pleasant reading!

BARRIE ROBERTS is a paranormal investigator and internationally published thriller writer. For eight years he has taught a course in Birmingham on Ghosts and Unsolved Mysteries.

INTRODUCTION

T IS NOW FIVE YEARS since I began collecting ghost stories. At that time, I was firmly convinced that ghosts did not exist. A few of my friends had tales of strange experiences, but I was sure that they were putting a supernatural interpretation on a natural event.

Then at the beginning of the 1990's, I happened to come across a collection of Victorian local ghost stories in Redditch library. Philip Davis, the local history librarian, agreed with me that it was a shame to hide them away and that they should be made public, and he persuaded me to update and publish them. I was amazed when these paranormal experiences began pouring in from all sides. Who can read, say, the Kempsey or the Astwood Bank story and not believe in spirits? I now believe, without a doubt, that poltergeists and ghosts do exist and that science doesn't have all the answers.

Of course, it would be nice if every apparition were seen by more than one person but unfortunately, life is not so convenient and many of these reports are of single sightings. I hope, however, that readers will be able to spot similarities between one story and another which gives credence to each. There are plenty of dark monks and phantom footsteps. White ladies originate from pools at Grafton, Feckenham and Hanbury. Barrels of beer are mysteriously turned off at the Old Mug House in Claines, Redditch Football Club and Bottles Wine Bar in Worcester. The coarse fabric of the apparition's clothing is noticed at Drakes Broughton, Great Witley and Redditch Shopping Centre. A shower of sparks herald the arrival of an apparition at Leominster and at Redditch Football Ground. Many of the narratives have what Barrie Roberts describes as 'the whiff of a poltergeist'. And so on.

I hope this is a book which everyone, even the sceptics, will find interesting and – most of all – enjoyable.

An * in the text shows that this is not their real name. If anyone has an interesting paranormal anecdote, Anne Bradford at Hunt End Books would be interested to hear it. All stories are checked with the narrator who can remain anonymous if he or she wishes.

WORCESTERSHIRE TOWNS

WORCESTER

 OUR OF WORCESTER'S PAST BISHOPS have become saints which is more than from any other cathedral. This is symbolic of a lovely city, where the walls of the cathedral rise from the river Severn and the towers climb still further skyward. Worcester has a long tradition of miracles, visions, apparitions and…ghosts.

To quote Bill Gwillam, 'There was a Bishop at Worcester before there was a king of England'. The first one to be canonised was Egwin who was appointed in 692. He founded Evesham on a vision, more of that later in the Evesham section. Saint Dunstan, the iron-worker who claimed to have held the devil by his nose with blacksmith's pincers, became bishop in 957, followed by the learned Saint Oswald in 959. Oswald rebuilt the cathedral but unfortunately, it only stood for eighty years before it was razed to the ground by Hardicanute, the son of King Canute. He had sent his tax inspectors to Worcester but the citizens had shown their disapproval by murdering them, so Worcester had been sacked in reprisal.

The cathedral rose again from the ruins when Saint Wulstan became bishop in 1062 and part of his church still remains as the crypt. Wulston was bishop during the Norman invasion (1066), and the Norman Archbishop of Canterbury summoned Wulstan in order to take his bishopric from him. However, according to tradition, Wulstan laid his bishop's staff on the tomb of Saint Edward 'whereat the stones of the sepulchre broke asunder' so that no man could remove the staff except Wulstan, and by this strange episode he held on to his bishopric. There are many citizens of Worcester walking around today who would not be here were it not for Wulstan, as he was able to bring about a smooth takeover by the Normans from the Saxons, whereas elsewhere there was fighting and bloodshed. Many miracles were performed at the tombs of Oswald and Wulstan and, during the thirteenth century these were visited by thousands of pilgrims, providing a handsome income for the Cathedral.

Worcester was an important town even before records began. Its position on the River Severn and the River Teme, including a piece of high ground near a ford (where the cathedral now stands), gave it important strategic and trading advantages. During Saxon times it was the capital of the kingdom of the Hwiccae and in later years it was one of England's major medieval cities. King John, who died in 1216, left instructions that he should be buried in Worcester Cathedral, with Saint Wulstan on one side and Saint Oswald on the other. In this way he hoped to slip into heaven unnoticed between the two saints. Prince Arthur, the much-loved son of Henry VII, was also laid to rest here in 1502

The Vikings swept up the River Severn to raid Worcester so frequently that a huge wall was built round the city in about 890. The story goes that one of the raiders tried to carry off a huge church bell but it was too heavy for him, he was left behind by his companions and caught by the townsfolk. They flayed him alive and a piece of his skin was nailed to the cathedral door for centuries, in fact there are people alive today who can remember seeing it. The city was again plundered by Owain Glyndwr in 1405 who led the Welsh in a bloody uprising against the English, 'without sparing neither child nor church'.

Few visitors know that as they approach the entrance porch on the northern wall, they are walking over innumerable human bones which lie just below ground level. Alongside this wall ran the charnel-house where bones were deposited. No-one knows where the bones have come from, some are thought to be the remains of monks, others could be the bodies of Puritans and Cavaliers killed at the battle of Worcester in 1651.

More fighting went on in Worcestershire during the civil war (1642 – 1651) than in any other county, and Worcester suffered every year between 1642 and 1646 and was beseiged by the Parliamentarians in 1646.

The last great battle of 1651 was fought mainly on the flat scrubland around Powick bridge, but fighting also took place elsewhere. Defensive lines ran from Fort Royal to the great south gate of the city at Sidbury, only a few yards from the cathedral. The gate was the scene of great slaughter and after the battle, bodies were stacked up against it.

No wonder the Barley Mow, in Sidbury, is haunted. The pub has a Victorian frontage but the back is much older. It was kept by George and Angela Barrett from 1971 until 1992. The Barretts have four daughters and Michelle, the eldest, has the most vivid memories of their strange resident.

Fred and the Barley Mow

Michelle Barrett

When my parents first moved there, we had a club room on the first floor, but later we had it converted into a living room. This is where our ghost lived. He was a friendly entity and I think he was attracted to people because he liked to make his presence known. He was continually opening the club room door and we could hear his footsteps in there, they were definitely a man's footsteps and they sounded as if they were walking on lino. We grew quite fond of our ghost and we called him Fred.

There was a bloke in the pub who said that he didn't believe in ghosts and didn't believe that Fred kept opening the club room door. This particular door had a hole in it for the convenience of the Buffaloes who used the room, they liked to be able to look out and see who was knocking before they opened up. It also meant that you could put your hand through the hole and check that the door was locked. Anyway, the next time we had a meeting in there, this bloke sat on the stairs for ten minutes to see if the door would open. It remained closed but as he turned away to come down the stairs, laughing at us, the door slowly swung open.

Mrs Barrett, a sensible, down-to-earth woman, gives more details.

There's no doubt that the place was haunted. As you worked in the kitchen downstairs you would feel that someone was walking behind you. Bottles would rattle violently for no reason. We would often find that the gas in the cellar had been turned off. Outside was a built-in yard and somebody came in once and said that there was a whirlwind in the yard and everything was flying round.

Once I was in the cellar and the door slammed shut and I couldn't open it. Fortunately, there is another way out so I was able to go round and come out the other way. That has never happened before or since. It was very eerie.

My husband was showing somebody out late one night and there were only two people there, my husband and this other person. Suddenly, the visitor said, 'There's somebody behind you'. He said that the ghost appeared to be going down steps behind the bar but there are no steps. He said that the ghost looked like a long-haired yobbo but we have assumed that it was a Cavalier because of Worcester's association with the Royalists.

The battle recreated

Across the road from the cathedral is the Commandery which was heavily involved in the battle of Worcester. The Duke of Hamilton was carried in here with an injured leg. Two days later, while doctors and friends were arguing whether or not his leg should be amputated, he died. The Commandery stands on the site of a hospital built by Saint Wulstan, the staff were called, 'Commanders', hence its name. It is now a museum in which the battle of Worcester is recreated with models and a video. The present building is about 500 years old; dark, carved wood is much in evidence, the windows are small and an occasional piece of stained glass catches the light. This is the perfect venue for a haunting and many visitors feel an inexplicable chill in certain places. One evening a few years ago, a local eminent businessman arrived early for a meeting in the Solar, a large room on the first floor. After about fifteen minutes, the receptionist on duty was surprised to hear him come crashing down the stairs and as he rushed past her and out through the main doors he called that he was never going back into that room again. To this day he will not reveal what he saw.

Mrs Hazel★ travelled from Stafford with her twelve-year old daughter. She entered the Solar and:

> As I walked towards the fireplace I suddenly felt extremely cold and I had this strange feeling that someone else was there. I looked at my daughter and noticed that she had gone very pale but I didn't say anything about it at the time and waited for her to tell me about it. Later that day she said, 'I felt that there was something very strange in that room. When I was standing by the fireplace I felt that something was there, watching me'. So you can see it wasn't just me and my imagination. Both of us felt it.

The battle of Worcester was so terrible that Charles vowed that never again would he lead an army to war. He had been persuaded to visit Scotland and raise an army to overthrow Oliver Cromwell, who was becoming increasingly unpopular. 16,000 Scots clashed with 28,000 English and at the end of the day, 3,000 men lay dead or dying. Charles watched the battle from the tower and briefly joined in the fighting at Sidbury but when it became obvious that he was on the losing side, he made his escape and became one of the most hunted men in history for six weeks until he was able to reach France.

The battle has left Worcestershire with a legacy of ghostly Roundheads and Cavaliers such as this Roundhead at Stoulton.

The long-faced roundhead

Eleanor Rudge*

It all started when my sister brought a cat home in 1985 or 1986. One day, the cat went ballistic at the French window, with her teeth bared, for no reason that we could understand. Later, we discovered that the French window had once been the front door of the house.

I happened to glance out of the kitchen window one afternoon and there was our ghost! He's just in the one area of the garden, in the side part where we discovered that there was once an old front door – I don't know if that's significant. He's not solid, more see-through, and he's a funny grey colour. You can't see his hair because he has a hat on, neither can you see his features because his head is bowed. You can tell that he's very glum from the way his head hangs down. He doesn't move, he just stands there with his hands by his side. His feet aren't on the floor yet he's not hanging in the air.

Sometimes you don't see him but you can sense that he's there. I know that sounds silly and I can only add that our window cleaner has had the same sensation. He kept turning round and looking back over his shoulder and he remarked, 'I feel that somebody's watching me'.

My mother and I have only ever seen him in that one corner but my friend's brother saw him outside the gate. This brother was on his way to pick his sister up from a party, which took him past our house. He remarked to my friend, 'Eleanor's mum and dad are having a fancy dress party, there's a soldier standing outside their gate'. When they asked me about it I had to embarrassingly explain that it was our resident ghost. The brother saw the ghost on the other side of the fence in the road. We haven't seen the soldier there, maybe because we don't look for him.

Eleanor's mother adds:

I can't tell whether the apparition in my garden is a World War II soldier or a Roundhead. However, tradition has it that Cromwell gathered his troops at the bottom of Stoulton Hill, Hawbridge, which is half a mile away, I therefore suspect that it may be the latter. The apparition has a hat with a regular round crown and a short brim. He's wearing some kind of uniform which is neither blue nor khaki, more a type of grey. As for his feet – up to his knees the uniform is closely fitted – he is wearing socks or puttees, then his trousers bulge above the knee. His head is always bowed, he looks worn out and very depressed – totally knackered!

Each year, I see him several times over several months but only in my garden and only during the summer. He usually puts in an appearance when I'm gardening but once I was cleaning the windows and I noticed his reflection in the glass. I turned round but no-one was there. He's never more than six feet away and because his head is bowed I've no idea what his age might be. He never moves but just stands there and disappears after a couple of minutes.

No-one who has seen him felt afraid, we never feel he is a threat, he's very benign. I feel sorry for him and I wish I could find out who he is because he looks so sad. We've all spoken to him but there's no reply – it's like talking to your husband!

The question is, why should the roundhead look so sad? At the great battle of Worcester he was on the victorious side! However, by a strange quirk of fate the first fight of the civil war in 1642 was also fought at Powick Bridge, as well as the last great, decisive battle. An equestrian detachment of Roundheads accidentally bumped into a detachment of Cavaliers headed by Prince Rupert at Powick Bridge. It was little more than a skirmish but about 50 soldiers were killed and the Roundheads fled. Perhaps the apparition took part in this earlier battle.

Goings-on in Friar Street

Worcester has always been, first and foremost, a Cathedral city. Its reputation for religious, musical and academic excellence, not to mention its prosperity, attracted other religions to settle nearby, among them various orders of Friars. The Friars were members of the established (Roman Catholic) church who depended upon alms for their living and they were distinguished by the colour of their habits. The Grey Friars (Franciscans) were the first to arrive in about 1239 and they settled east of Friar Street. The Black Friars (Dominicans) came in 1347, their house stood by Broad Street and Angel Lane. There is now no sign of the friaries and chapels built by them but they appear to have left behind a series of strange entities. The Talbot Hotel, on the corner of Sidbury and Friar Street, has a ghostly fat, black, sleek cat which puts in an appearance from time to time. The Cardinal's Hat, almost opposite, has a room on the first floor which becomes inexplicably hot, reputedly after a maid was burned to death there several hundred years ago (see Midland Ghosts and Hauntings). Further along Friar Street is the Bottles Wine Bar.

Spirits in bottles

Bottles Wine Bar, Worcester

Despite the trendy name and plate glass windows, a substantial part of this building is known to have existed as long ago as 1408. It stood at the north-western
edge of Greyfriars Friary and has been used chiefly as a bakery and baker's shop.
Over the centuries parts have been extended and adjacent buildings assimilated

so that it is now a charming hotchpotch of oak beams, unexpected steps, uneven floors and rooms that disappear round dark corners. To the rear is a tiny yard, enclosed by buildings but open to the sky, and leading off this is the small dry store and a larger cellar which has recently been refrigerated.

In the autumn of 1994 a new member of staff started work at Bottles and on the Thursday afternoon she was left on her own to mind the bar. To the right of the bar and almost behind it is a flight of wooden steps, leading to a balcony above. She was tidying up one or two odds and ends, half-listening to the background music, when suddenly she was surprised to hear slow, heavy footsteps ascending the wooden steps and walking along the balcony. She came out of bar and turned round to look up at the staircase to see who was there, and to her horror, found it quite empty. Fortunately, her boyfriend worked in a shop a few doors down the road so she telephoned him and insisted that he stayed with her for the remainder of the afternoon. She then left and refused to come back.

Nicky has worked at Bottles for three years and was appointed manager at the beginning of 1994. She says that all the staff hear the footsteps but they don't bother about them.

Sometimes the footsteps just go up the staircase, at other times they go as far as the cleaning cupboard in the front room. They are just a minor event in a series of strange happenings here. We seem to have a poltergeist which manifests itself in the stairs and balcony but most of all, in the refrigerated storeroom outside. We have also had some problems in the dry store, where we keep the vegetables, and in the yard.

Until recently the poltergeist has not been much of a problem. We did have strange things happening but they were very few and far between. My first experience of it came at the end of one night when I had only been here a few days. As a rookie (newest member of staff), instead of sitting with the others and having a drink after we had closed, I had to sweep and clean the bar floor. I finished mopping and went outside for only a few seconds to take the mop. When I came back all the buckets, which had been behind the bar, were dragged into the middle of the bar. I thought someone was playing a joke on me but everyone laughed at the idea that they would do such a stupid thing. In any case the floor was wet and if anyone had walked on it I would have seen their footsteps. No-one had heard anything either and buckets are quite noisy items to move. I didn't think much about it, I was more annoyed than anything.

Then just before Christmas 1994, we had the cellar out the back fitted with huge refrigerators, previously it had been the store room for wine and bottled beers. In order to do this it was necessary to drill the walls almost the whole length of the building and fit piping, which runs from the cellar, across the balcony and down into the bar. These alterations seemed to start the poltergeist off. That's when things really began to happen.

A day or two later I went into the cellar and was literally in there for just two seconds. When I came out there was a crate of bottles right in the doorway, in fact I tripped over them. Almost the next day I saw, with my own eyes, a keg in the dry store fall over, roll across the floor then stand up again. It was unbelievable. It hadn't hit anything. Then, about a week after the refrigerators had been installed, they failed to work and we had to get the engineer out. He said that he couldn't understand it, someone had turned the refrigerator off but it couldn't have been any of the staff because it's quite a complicated operation and you needed a special spanner to do it which, of course, we didn't have.

We keep a set of frying pans in the kitchen, all stacked one on top of the other, and one morning about this time, I arrived at work to find that the pans were stacked behind the front door. I had to push them with the door in order to get in. The strange thing is that we have an alarm which is activated by any movement and the pans managed to get from one end of the very long bar to the other without setting off the alarm. We were very busy, it was just before Christmas, and we found these incidents very frustrating.

Everything went fairly quiet until July but then events began to snow-ball. Since then, hardly a week has gone by without something happening. It came to a head on 21 September 1995. It began just as a normal Thursday evening, Gemma and I were on duty and two of our regular customers were in the bar. Then Gemma went out to the refrigerated cellar to begin cleaning. She set up the transparent hose (known as the Bodding-ton line), putting the free end in a bucket of cleaning fluid and, to prevent it from falling out of the bucket she held it in place by a metal wedge which is so heavy that you can only just lift it. When she went back to check it half an hour later the line had been completely removed from the bucket and was lying six feet away with the metal wedge on top. It would have been impossible for it to fall like that. She set it up again, very carefully this time, and went back a short time later. Again, the line had been removed and was lying with the metal wedge exactly as before.

On the same night, I went into the dry store to get some jacket pota-toes and found that the box of potatoes had completely disappeared. We always keep the box in the same place and they were simply not there. Ten minutes later I went out of the dry store and the door slammed shut. We struggled to open the door but discovered that the door had managed to lock itself so we went to get the key. I was so frightened that the next time I went in there, one of the customers came with me and as he approached the store all the hairs on his arms stood upright. We opened the door and there was one potato in the middle of the floor. I grabbed it and ran. Locking up time was an hour later which meant that I had to go out the back again. When I opened the door of the dry store I was amazed to see that the box of potatoes had reappeared in the exact place that it was missing from, but it was upside down with potatoes all over the floor. Gemma and I were very, very frightened.

One Friday night, one of the staff had left his bike out in the yard. There's always a strange wind in that yard, it must be some kind of wind tunnel. At about 10.30 that evening I went out the back, noticed the bike outside and thought it would have been better under cover in the cellar, but I decided not to move it. An hour later this person went out to get his bike to find that it had been moved into the cellar. None of us had been out and there is no public access to that area – it's surrounded by high walls.

Gemma, the Duty Manager:

Nicky's last incident shows the way in which whatever-it-is reads our minds. It often does that. I was closing up one night and I said to Nicky, 'I'm going to turn the CD off now!' As I said it, the CD turned itself off! It was off for about ten seconds then it turned itself on again. On another occasion we were thinking of playing a practical joke on one of the staff. Although he's over six feet tall he's quite nervous of our ghost, so we thought that we would arrange some of the furniture half way down the stairs, as if the ghost had thrown it down. In the end, we decided not to do this – we thought it would be too scary. Two days later when we turned up for work this is exactly what had happened – the furniture was halfway down the stairs.

The poltergeist seems to have an intelligence. Not only does it read our minds, it also does something that it knows you are soon going to see, like the night it interfered with the Boddington line. It knew we would be going back to check the line.

Sometimes, an incident is quite amusing – there was the time I was sitting on the loo when I heard someone tapping on the wall, it sounded as if they were tapping on tiles with a key. Occasionally, it can be quite frightening. I was going up the steps to the balcony one night when I heard a howl right behind me. I thought a cat had got in but when I turned round, nothing was there. Sometimes, when I go into the yard I hear a young woman give a terrible scream. It only lasts for a second or two but it's quite chilling.

However, most of the time the poltergeist is simply a nuisance. It messes about with the electrics, the lights flash and we have that many light bulbs going all the time. Just a few minutes ago I went into the dry store and before I could switch the light on, it had flashed on and gone off again. There's a large walk-in cupboard off the storeroom where the heating controls are. One night, we couldn't get the heating to work. Just as we walked back through it went on and off again.

One Saturday night about eight weeks ago, everyone had gone home and Nicky was the last person here, so she swept up and had about two dustpans full of dirt and debris. When she came to get the dustpan and brush, they weren't there, so she swept the debris to the end of the bar and put the broom on top of it, leaning the broom against the wall, intending to deal with it on Monday morning. On the Sunday, I happened to be passing and when I looked in through the glass door everything was in a mess. The floor was covered with debris and the broom was lying in the middle of the floor. The rubbish was everywhere, there was no way it could have been caused by a draught. I was a bit surprised that Nicky should leave the bar in such a state and I came in and swept up. Also, a CD was playing quietly but I didn't think twice about it, I just thought Nicky had forgotten to switch the CD player off. The next day, Nicky said that she was certain she had switched it off and she pointed out that even if she hadn't, the machine switches itself off after five CDs. Another inexplicable fact was that when I turned the machine off, the CD was playing quietly and when we turned it on again the next morning the music was blaring out. No-one had touched the volume control.

Opposite the bar is a line of six small dining tables and every table has a lighted candle in the centre. I was standing behind the bar last week when I saw each candle go out, one by one, as if someone was walking past the tables, snuffing each one out as he went past.

I was sceptical about these things until I came here. I've now changed my mind!

Nicky adds a final comment:

We're used to the poltergeist, it's become part of our daily routine. We often find things in strange places that nobody has moved. This morning we found a box in the cellar that had been locked away in the storeroom. We're very tidy and organised and if anything is not exactly where it should be somebody notices it straight away and asks you about it. This is the only place I've worked at where, if you move anything, you have to justify it and explain why you did it!

Elegant Worcester

By the 1700s the citizens began to feel that peace had, at last, come to Worcester. The buildings in and around Greenhill, Sidbury, Foregate Street, Tything and Barbourne had been demolished to make way for the defences of the Battle of Worcester and the area had lain derelict for more than fifty years, but now a cautious rebuilding began. This was the start of the Georgian period with its beautifully proportioned, elegant houses. Bishop Maddox, in 1743, said that the city was 'of some beauty and rising importance'. The rebuilding of Foregate Street began in 1730 and by the end of the century the street was said to be the finest in England. Among the local businessmen living there was John Dent, whose company had manufactured fine gloves since before the fifteenth century. He eventually became rich enough to buy Sudeley Castle.

Trade flourished and Worcester Porcelain arrived in 1751, when a deed of partnership was signed by fourteen gentlemen to form a company to make porcelain. Worcestershire sauce arrived in the first half of the nineteenth century with a recipe brought back from India by Lord Sandys. The original premises were in Broad Street.

Danger in the churchyard

During this period of redevelopment, a strange happening occurred in the cathedral churchyard, detailed in Bill Gwillam's *Old Worcester, People and Places*.

In 1718, a young servant girl, Mary Bentall, was dismissed from her post as maidservant at Little Wenlock and went to work for a widow who owned a public house at Sidbury. She was subject to poltergeist activity and it is said that stones fell through the air, narrowly missing her as she worked. Because of this, she was dismissed and went to work at another public house in the College churchyard. Again, 'stones, brickbats and tiles flew about her like hailshots, to the great amazement of the family'. The poor girl was distraught and talked about suicide.

Matters came to a head when she was accused of stealing a silk apron. The magistrate asked her if she had some great crime on her conscience, such as murder, to cause this activity. She said that at her previous employment at Little Wenlock, her mistress had confessed to her that she had murdered her husband.

The maid was imprisoned for the theft of the apron.

A curious fact is that ever since that time, the churchyard has been troubled by falling bricks.

At a house in Edgar Street which backed on to the churchyard, a housemaid was killed in 1804 by a falling chimney stack. Six years later the chimney of the same house was struck by lightning, burning the owner's hands, eyebrows and stockings. In the 1960's the chimney stack of the White Hart fell at almost exactly the same spot, killing another young girl.

A royal ghost

Worcester was visited by the rich and famous. In 1802 Horatio Nelson stayed at the Hop Pole Inn (on the corner of Foregate Street and Shaw Street) accompanied by his lover, Lady Hamilton. She was shunned by the local ladies whom Nelson later referred to as, 'Those damned glover women!'. In 1830 the inn was visited by the more respectable Princess Victoria.

One of its better-known residents was Mrs Henry Wood, the author of popular melodramatic Victorian novels, who was born in Sidbury in 1814 and set many of her novels in Worcester. Six million of her books had been sold by 1914. She wrote *East Lynne,* the last line of which is the well-known, 'Dead, and never called me mother!'.

Every fashionable city had to have its theatre and the Theatre Royal was erected in Angel Street in 1779. It has hosted most of the great Victorian artists, including the Kembles, Mrs Siddons and Edmund Kean. It was rebuilt in 1877 but demolished in the 1960s to make way for a car showroom. Like every first class theatre it had a ghost (or a collection of ghosts), described here by a well-known Flamenco dancer and native of Worcester, Delphine.

The old theatre Royal was an eerie place, but I loved it. I was in pantomime there in the 1955/56 season when they did Cinderella, and that was when I saw the apparitions.

To get into the back of the theatre you had to go down this long corridor on the left-hand side which led from the main street to the stage door. There were only three lights along the whole length and in those days they were still the old-fashioned gas lamps. As I went into this corridor, I saw three figures walking along in front of me, because of the poor light I could only see dark shapes. I called to them 'Hey wait for me!' but as they reached the stage door they passed straight through without it opening. That was not the only time I saw them – by the time the pantomime season was over

I had seen them three times.

This was one of the last of the Theatre Royal's pantomimes as the theatre was closed only a year or two later.

The three figures I saw could have been a trick of the lights, but they were always in front of me, never behind. I like to think that I saw this, because I have always thought that these strange things (here and in other parts of the world) seem as if they have been recorded on television, on a box made for this purpose. I saw myself on the TV the other week in a film made 25 years ago and I felt that I was seeing a ghost dancing from the past.

Plagues and epidemics

The 18th and 19th centuries were times of peace and prosperity. Only one major potential disaster remained – epidemics.

A deserted area at the end of Angel Place (which later became the market place) was a reminder of the outbreak of bubonic plague in 1637. This was the site of a plague pit containing the remains of the most of the 1,551 victims. Although by the eighteenth and nineteenth century the plague had died out, there were plenty of other epidemics. 1847/8 brought a severe outbreak of cholera. Typhoid broke out in 1886 (15 deaths) and again in 1892 (14 deaths). 1986 brought 127 cases of diptheria with 16 deaths when schools were closed for as long as nine weeks. An improved water supply would have improved the health of the city but the citizens preferred to build churches rather than sewers. As late as 1846 there was only one short sewer in the whole town. In one very respectable shop, the WC drained into a brick-covered pit in the cellar and occasionally, the bricks were removed and the effluent baled out into the street.

The next story by John Ludlow* sounds very much as if it occurred during the time of an epidemic. If a woman came knocking on your door and you suspected that her family were suffering from a highly-infectious disease, would you let her in?

My mother lives in Bath Road, which is the A38 as it comes from the centre of Worcester. Her present house is about a hundred years old but before that it was an isolated farm worker's cottage, one up and one down. She doesn't like talking about her ghost but I have heard it many times so I can tell you all about it. About midnight, there comes a frantic knocking on the brick wall, but the knocking doesn't sound as if it's on brick, it sounds as if it's on wood. After about ten minutes, it begins to get slower and weaker and starts going down the wall, eventually stopping at floor

level. It occurs almost every night in the summer time then during the
autumn it tails off a bit.

Originally there was a door where the wall is now and the legend is that
sometime during the last century, the husband of a couple who lived nearby
was taken ill. The wife rushed across the fields to this cottage to try and
get help. She knocked on the door but no-one answered it and she died on
the doorstep.

Oddity at the Oddfellows

The Insurance Companies and Friendly Societies were there to give assistance
in sickness or poverty. One of the largest was the Order of the Oddfellows,
founded early in the 1700s. The Oddfellow's Hall in New Street has recently been
put to a number of rather undignified uses, including a playgroup which happily
moved to other premises in 1990. The playgroup supervisor was Mrs Joan Bond.

One morning in about 1983 I stood in the kitchen talking to the cook, Lily,
when a little old lady came into the rear of the kitchen and went up the
stairs behind Lily. As Lily had her back to the stairs, she didn't see her.

I said, 'Oh, someone's just gone up the stairs!' Lily said, 'I wonder who
that was?' I offered to go up and see who she was and what she wanted. I
went up and had a good look round but no-one was there.

We told the lady who did the cleaning, Joan, and she said, 'What did she
look like?' I said that she was elderly, very tiny and bent over. Her hair was
in a bun and she was wearing a maroon cardigan with a long black skirt. I

couldn't see her features because she was so bent over. Joan said, 'She sounds like the lady who used to have a flat up there but she died years ago!'.

Well! What do you make of that! There was never a flat when I was there, it was just full of rubbish!

I wasn't afraid at all – well I didn't think she was a ghost. She looked quite normal.

The story was covered by *Berrows Worcester Journal* (22 January 1993) who interviewed the Hall's secretary, Tom Byrne. Tom said that he was not surprised by the story and added, 'People often report strange noises here, so we might well have a ghost, but I have never seen one myself'.

The curious case of the woman on the stairs in Worcester's ancient Oddfellows Hall is to feature in a collection of ghost stories compiled by a county writer.

Related by Mrs Joan Bond, of Elbury Park, Worcester, the tale of the disappearing old woman was just one of a score of stories told to author Anne Bradford by readers of Berrow's Worcester Journal.

They included tales of spontaneous combustion at Great Witley, a mysterious tobacco smell in a house at Upton Snodsbury and a weird experience on a haunted highway at Bromsgrove.

The Oddfellows Hall in New Street was where Mrs Bond saw an apparition of a grey haired old woman.

It is one of the city's oldest buildings, a rambling collection of rooms, staircases and passages, dating in part from the 16th century.

About 10 years ago, Mrs Bond was running a day nursery there.

"I was in the big kitchen talking to the cook and I saw a little old lady go up the stairs, hanging on to the rail," she said.

"She looked like a typical old fashioned granny.. Her hair was pulled back into a bun and she was wearing a maroon jumper and a long black skirt.

"I didn't think I was seeing a ghost. She looked real enough to me. I wondered what she wanted and I went after her, because there was nothing up there apart from some store rooms. "But there sas no sign of her and nowhere she could have gone without coming back down the same stairs."

The cleaner later told Mrs Bond that her old lady sounded like a woman who previousy lived in a flat there, but was now dead.

Oddfellows secretary Tom Byre was not surprised by the story. "people often report strange noises here, so we might well have a ghost, but I have never seen one myself," he said.

A homeless spook

Worcester found itself at war again in 1939 with the worst air-raid occurring in 1940. The second half of the twentieth century brought other problems such as unemployment, a rising crime rate – and homelessness.

The Young Men' Christian Association in Henwick Road caters for the homeless and divorced of all ages. It has sixty single rooms with three set aside for women. The next anecdote from Charles Wright* takes place in the 1960's when the Worcester YMCA sometimes catered for trainees but it has now changed its policy and only accommodates those with special needs.

I was a trainee with the Midland Electricity Board in the 1960's and they put us up at the YMCA in Henwick Road, Worcester. I don't know what the YMCA is like now, but in those days it was very basic. There was no en suite and you had to walk down a series of dimly lit corridors to reach the communal bathroom. There were fifteen of us with two or three sharing each room.

Being teenagers, we were out late at night burning the midnight oil and then when we got back we had a midnight game of cards. I'm the sort who likes to have a wash and clean my teeth before I go to sleep at night so at 1.30 in the morning off I set, down the long dark corridors, with my towel over my shoulder and toothbrush in hand. As I neared the communal bathroom I could see that my way was being blocked by a large, immaculately-dressed bloke who was leaning on one arm against the door post. He had a black cloak tied at the neck, and a strange suit with a grandad type collar, a small tie and a Quaker hat. He had cold, staring eyes and he stared straight at me. He wouldn't move and I had to duck under his arm to get into the bathroom. As I went under his arm I froze and felt very cold. When I turned round he had vanished.

I couldn't wait to get back into my room. That was one time in my life when I skipped the wash.

The vergers story

This last narrative comes not from the city centre, but from one of those beautiful old churches of Norman origin in the Worcester diocese. I came across it quite by accident when I asked for permission to take photographs and mentioned to the Verger that I was looking for ghost stories. This tale is so curious that I first thought I was misunderstanding it.

I have always thought that my aunt was an angel. My brother and I were abandoned when we were small and my aunt and uncle took us in and brought us up. We lived in a comfortable, pre-war house not far from here. When we were in our late teens my aunt died but my uncle, brother and I worked well together, we were a team. After another eight or nine years my uncle died.

It was after my uncle's death that my aunt began putting in an appearance. I am a Christian, and I believe that we have spirits all round us all the time, some good, some bad, so I am not unduly alarmed when I see her. In fact, I feel a very peaceful sensation. I believe that my aunt visits us because she is worried about us. I suppose it is very nice of her to worry about us and come back. What I should do is to talk to her, to reassure her and tell her that she is not to worry, we are alright, but I must admit I am too apprehensive to do that. I don't want her to know that I can see her and I just ignore her.

I see her sitting on my bed at night most nights when I go to bed but I just turn over and go to sleep. I know that she is there watching me during the day because I feel this cold sensation just a little way from my face. People tell me it must be a draught but how can you have a draught when the door is shut and the windows are closed? My brother sees her more often than I do, he is very sensitive to this sort of thing. He, too, ignores her, we say that she has had her life, now we are going to get on with ours.

Two or three times she has been joined by my uncle and once they even brought the dog! There was my aunt, uncle and the dog all crowded into my little bedroom!

We have had the house blessed twice, not so much for our sake but for hers, to send her on to her final resting place. Each time, she has gone for a few months but then she's back.

I believe that we live with these spirits all round us, sometimes we see them, sometimes we don't, some spirits are good, others are bad and throughout life we gradually move towards the spirit world until we become part of it at death.

BROMSGROVE

They say my verse is sad: no wonder;
Its narrow measure spans
Tears of eternity and sorrow,
Not mine, but man's.[†]

 LFRED EDWARD HOUSMAN is generally thought to have come from Shropshire because of his well-known poem, 'A Shropshire Lad' but in actual fact he was born at Fockbury, Bromsgrove in 1859, as his statue in the centre of Bromsgrove testifies. He was educated at Bromsgrove School and left for St John's College Oxford, later becoming professor of Latin at Cambridge and one of England's best-selling poets.

The M5 and M42 now converge a quarter of a mile to the east of Fockbury but in Housman's days the village would have been a peaceful rural backwater, full of provincial gossip. Housman would have no doubt heard of the story of Battle Brook which now runs south along the M5, locals say that this is so-called after a skirmish between the Roundheads and Cavaliers. Although this is not documented, it could have taken place as the civil war was one of minor skirmishes rather than great battles, many of which went unrecorded. A pale young lady dressed in white is said to wander along the stream when the evening begins to fall, looking for her lover who was killed in the fighting.

Housman would also have heard the old story that a minstrel was murdered in a field opposite the Clock House at Fockbury and on stormy nights you can hear the fiddle being played.

Housman spent his teenage years in the Clock House, but the following incident took place in later years when the house was occupied by Colonel Morcom and his family.

The rose garden

Sarah Brampton*

I suppose that I have always believed in ghosts because my mother saw one when she was young and often used to tell me about it.

In the 1920's she was a housemaid at the Clock House which has now

---

[†]Published in More Poems (1936), Housman

been pulled down but it was near to the present aerial. The site is very old and that house replaced an even older one. She always said that the rose garden felt strange and she avoided going there if she could. However, one day she and another two or three housemaids had finished their work early and the lady of the house said to them, 'Why don't you go outside for a bit of fresh air – go and have a turn in the rose garden', so they went outside and there was the ghost. Another girl could see her as well as my mother but the other two housemaids couldn't see her. My mother said how beautiful she was. For two or three minutes they stood there, watching her floating along, in and out of the rose beds. She had long fair hair and a long silky dress that floated in the air. She shimmered from head to foot – mother remarked to me that the Star Trek crew materialising looked much the same. Then she gave a final violent shimmer, as if a gust of wind had caught her, and she disappeared.

The jovial hunter

Housman is not the only bard of Bromsgrove. In the British Museum is a ballad written in the time of Henry VIII about Sir Ryalas the Jovial Hunter, who is, so the ballad says, buried in Bromsgrove church. While out hunting Sir Ryalas met an old woman who begged him to save her from a boar but the old woman turned out to be a wicked witch and the boar was her son. Sir Ryalas chopped the witch in two.

Glastonbury magic

For over a thousand years, Bromsgrove was a town of ironworkers and nailers. Although the shop fronts are Georgian, Victorian or modern, behind these facades some premises are so old that their date of origin is unknown. The manager of one of these shops is a Glastonbury lass. Whether or not she has brought some Glastonbury magic with her is anyone's guess. She lived quite a normal life until she was eighteen, then for absolutely no reason she began to have premonitions and to be sensitive to old buildings. This psychic awareness remains with her to this day.

Sometimes, I know what people are going to say and do next which my friends find very disconcerting. At other times I know who is going to be on the other end of a telephone line when they haven't been in touch for months. To give you an example, I had one friend who used to drop in without warning. Sometimes she'd say, 'I'll see you again in about three weeks' then a few days later I would start baking a cake and putting the kettle on. My husband would say, 'Don't be silly, she's not coming for a week or two yet' but then the doorbell would go and she would be standing on the doorstep.

I took over this shop in 1993 and I soon discovered that the shop had a reputation for being haunted. On one of my first days I was opening up the shop when an elderly man walked past and commented, 'Have you met the ghost yet?' I knew then that I would surely meet it sooner or later.

This shop has a third floor, a loft, used for storage. To get up there, you have to go up a ladder and open a trap door so there's no way anyone could get up there without our knowledge. We often hear footsteps walking across the floor of the loft. There's no mistaking the sound. One particular day we heard footsteps walk across the ceiling, then a tremendous thud, as if something heavy had been dropped. I went up to have a look but nothing had been disturbed. Some of the girls refuse to go up there, it's so spooky. Strange things are happening all the time, items go missing and turn up elsewhere. I complain bitterly because my pens keep making their way to the staff room but the girls protest that they're very careful not to go off with them. Several members of staff have this feeling that they are being watched, both in the office and in the loft.

I often catch sight of something out of the corner of my eye but when I turn round nothing is there. A few months ago, a young lad went to speak to me – he thought I was standing the other side of the counter but when he looked up the shop was empty. He didn't see the apparition clearly enough to describe it and didn't even know if it was male or female. He only knew that it was someone wearing black.

We've decided that it's male and we call him Frank. We often wonder if he's paid us a visit. Only this morning someone said, 'There's a customer in the shop' but when we went in no-one was there.

Frank doesn't cause any problem, he's more mischievous than anything. Some of the staff are sceptical, others are quite nervous. As for myself, I try not to think about it. It doesn't seem to stop people wanting to work here, it's a very happy shop.

The lavender lady

Ghosts are not always terrifying and the incident of the Clock House illustrates the fact that many people who have seen an apparition describe it as a very pleasant experience. The next story comes from one of a number of householders who have grown quite fond of their resident ghost.

I was very pregnant when we moved to this comfortable family home on the Old Birmingham Road and we had only been here two weeks when I had daughter number three. My husband worked over the other side of Birmingham so that I was alone in the house most of the time with three small children.

One day, I suddenly realised that this strong perfume was filling the house. I thought, 'Oh dear, one of the children has upset my lavender water!' I looked around but no lavender water had been spilt and the perfume disappeared as quickly as it came. This happened several times.

We had a very old dog and I noticed that his eyes used to move across the room as if he was watching someone walk across the room. Then my eldest daughter who was then about six or seven told me that a lady came to see her in the night. I thought, 'Oh dear, we have a ghost!'

Our house isn't all that old, it was built in the 1930's so I knew it would be quite easy to find out about previous residents. I began with an elderly neighbour who has lived in this area all her life. She told me that a man had built the house for his two spinster daughters. She added, 'Oh, you would have loved them, they were so nice. The one was a very busy little lady, always up to her eyes in good works, and the other was a very large lady, big-bosomed, the kind of person that everyone took their troubles to. Everywhere she went she carried a lacy hanky which had been kept in lavender so she always smelt of lavender!' I thought, 'Well, there's our lavender lady'. I wasn't afraid after that and quite enjoyed her little visits. As a fraught mum I would talk to her (an empty space) and always felt peaceful afterwards.

However, a few years ago we decided that the house wasn't big enough and my husband decided to extend the walls. It must have frightened our ghost away because we haven't smelt the lavender again.

See Midland Ghosts and Hauntings for more Bromsgrove ghost stories.

DROITWICH

HE FAIRY TALE TOWERS of the Chateau Impney Hotel rise to the south of the A38 as it joins the M5 near Droitwich. This is a French palace, built about 1875 by the Salt King, John Corbett, for his homesick wife whom he met in France. John was an ordinary Black Country working man but his family owned a little canal boat business and when they sold up, John had enough money to buy some run-down salt mines at Stoke Prior, near Droitwich. By improving the methods for extracting and refining the salt he became rich. The glorious Chateau did not bring him happiness, his wife left him in 1884. Furthermore, the workers resented the profits from their labours being used for this splendid palace and began various industrial actions which included a series of strikes.

John Corbett's success with Stoke Prior had sent the Droitwich salt mines into decline. John now turned his attention to Droitwich, building the Raven Hotel and turning the town into a popular spa.

Beneath Droitwich lies a great underground salt lake, for thousands of years the chief supply of salt in England. From earliest times wells have been sunk to obtain the salt which was valuable not only to flavour food but also to preserve it. An old legend says that the wells stopped up because the wood saints were upset at the amount of wood used in the fires to purify the salt. Saint Richard, a native of Droitwich, 'caused them by his prayers to flow again'. Ancient saltways radiate in all directions from Droitwich. The A38, which Paul Parsons had just turned off in the next story, is an old Roman road.

The phantom hitchhiker

This happened to me in 1975 and it was only about two years later that I heard the term 'phantom hitchhiker' and realised that this was what I had seen.

It was a nasty winter's night, the rain was lashing down and the trees were really going. Everything was on in my little minivan, the windscreen wipers, the blower, the lights, the radio. It was about one o'clock in the morning, the girlfriend and I had been to Worcester, then I had dropped her at her home in Droitwich and was going on to Stoke Prior, where I lived. I was on the A38, this was before the bypass was built, so I went past the Chateau Impney and went past the turn to Droitwich golf course. I began to go up the hill where there is a long bend to the left with trees, a hedge and a footpath. There was no traffic about.

I was about a quarter of a mile from the top of the hill when I saw somebody walking along on the side of the road, thumbing a lift. He appeared to me to be in his twenties and he was wearing a great big dark coat almost down to the ground with the collar pulled right up. 'I thought, I can't let the poor sod carry on in a night like this. Even if I only take him part of the way it will be a help!'. There was hardly any traffic about so I indicated left and stopped. I turned the radio off and reached over and opened the door. Nothing happened. I looked round and behind but I couldn't see anyone in the mirror.

I leaned over and got out the passenger side. This is quite easy and quick to do in a minivan. Nobody was there. I shut the passenger door and stood there in the pouring rain. It was very scarey, I can tell you. I shouted, 'Well, are you coming or aren't you?. Nobody appeared. Then I thought, 'Is there some crazy man lying behind the car?' I knelt down and looked, then I walked up and down the side of the road but still there was nothing. I said to myself, 'This is ridiculous! He couldn't have gone away. I was never more than a few feet from him and only took my eyes off him for a second or two'. I stood there for about fifteen seconds. Then I shouted, 'Well, you have bloody scared me!' or something like that and got back into the car. I was soaked through.

I drove off and went home as quickly as possible. It was a very frightening experience and the only thing I have to be thankful for was that the hitch-hiker didn't actually get into the car.

After that, I started going home a different way, on the Hanbury road.

Murder in Friar Street

The black and white Elizabethan walls of Priory House in Friar Street have been witness to a grisly murder. The Priory was the home of the wealthy and influential Carbury family and in the 1700's, it was arranged that Sir Richard Carbury should marry the only other direct descendent, his cousin Lucretia, but neither were very keen on the idea.

In 1738 Richard sailed with his regiment to America but when he returned home to claim his bride and his inheritance Lucretia arranged for him to sleep in a small room at the back of the house. There, she stabbed him to death. Sir Richard was buried in the grounds of Priory House where he puts in an occasional ghostly appearance.

The last recorded sighting was on April 14, 1875 when he terrified a guest,

Miss Porter, by materialising in her bedroom. Priory House is now used as offices and the site of Sir Richard's grave is under the town's ring road.

Priory House, Droitwich

The crying baby

A less spectacular but more recent story comes from a middle-aged couple who moved into Victoria Avenue in 1977 or 1978.

One evening, my husband wanted to watch something on the television that I wasn't particularly interested in, so off I went into another room to read my book. Suddenly, I noticed that I could hear a small child crying, a tired, whining cry. I went into my husband and said, 'Have you got a child crying on that telly?' He said that he hadn't. It lasted for about a minute then it faded away. It was really weird.

My late-teenage daughter was living with us at the time and I thought I had better tell her about it in case it happened again. Exactly a week later, my husband and I went out for the evening. When we arrived home my daughter was waiting for us. She said, 'Am I glad to see you two!' She had heard the child crying that evening at exactly the same time!

We only heard it just that twice. I asked around to see if a child had lived in the house before us but I never got to the bottom of it. If you mention the words 'crying baby' to my daughter now she'll shudder.

Top and whip

The final Droitwich anecdote is from April Pokorny, a young lady who lives in the area.

Late one summer afternoon in 1995, I was on my way home from college when, as I turned into Primsland Way, I saw a small boy playing in the middle of the road with a top and whip.

He was only a few yards away from me and he looked quite real except that he was hovering, he seemed to be playing on an invisible surface which was about 150 cms above the road itself. He was a lively little boy, kneeling down to place the top in the right position, jumping up to jerk the string out, then picking up the top and inspecting it, all on this surface above ground level.

Although he was quite small, he looked about nine years of age and he was predominantly brown, with brown trousers, cap, hair and eyes. The trousers were in a heavy, tweedy fabric and had a large red patch on the back. They were very baggy, reaching to below his knee – there was no doubt that they did not fit him properly. His shirt was off-white with a line of quilting running down each side of the buttons, and the top two buttons were undone. His feet were bare and he had some kind of rope or string tied round his right hand. He was quite scruffy, with dirt on his face and mucky hands. Although he had rosy cheeks, the lower half of his cheeks were drawn in, as if he was slightly undernourished, and he was very thin.

I was not at all frightened but quite fascinated by him. I stood and watched him for about five minutes, he was thoroughly enjoying himself and set the top spinning three or four times. He was obviously completely oblivious to me and didn't look at me at all. Then he turned and started walking away from me and that was when he faded away.

EVESHAM

N THE YEAR 702 a pig farmer, Eoves, wandered through a part of a forest which bordered on the Avon, looking for his pigs. When he reached a spot known as Hethomme, he saw a vision of three maidens, the middle one of exceptional beauty, who held a book in her hand and chanted passages in which her companions joined. Eoves rushed to tell Saint Egwin, Bishop of Worcester, of his experience.

Egwin was appointed Bishop of Worcester in 692 but because of his outspoken condemnation of evil, particularly marital infidelity, he made himself unpopular. He was banished from his See and sent for by the Pope. To mortify his enemies, he bound his legs and feet with chains and threw the key in the river Avon, declaring that he would walk to Rome in chains. When he had reached Rome, fish was served and there, inside the fish, was the key. After this miracle, Egwin's bishopric was, of course, restored.

Egwin had vowed that if he was reinstated to the Bishopric, he would found a church and priory and was wondering where that could be when Eoves arrived. Egwin visited the spot and found that he had a similar vision. This seemed to be divine guidance and a religious complex was built there. The name 'Hethomme' was eventually corrupted to Evesham.

Other miracles occurred during Egwin's lifetime and at his tomb after his death. The remains of the Abbey, its gateway and its churches can still be seen in the heart of Evesham town.

The Almonry museum

Next to the Abbey gatehouse is the lively Almonry museum, crammed with artefacts of every description. Richard Abbott lived with his family in the Almonry Museum when it was a private residence. He served in the Regular Army from 1939 to 1973, achieving the rank of Lieutenant Colonel.

Richard refers to Simon de Montford and the Battle of Evesham. To the ordinary people and the clergy, Simon de Montfort was a great hero. He had single-handedly forced Henry III to set up the very first parliament, with two knights from each shire and two leading citizens from each important town. However, the king and the barons continued to struggle for power and matters came to a head in 1265 at the Battle of Evesham. Simon and one of his sons were killed but his democratic vision lived after him and parliament has continued to meet ever since.

The Almonry Museum, Evesham

The ghost of Battle Well

My very first experience of the inexplicable was in 1931 when, as a boy of eleven, I went for a walk one hot summer afternoon round "The Squires", with my friend Eric. "The Squires" is a popular round-circuit walk of about three miles, starting and finishing at the town centre and embracing the Abbey Manor Estate, owned for generations by the Rudge family who were the Squires of Evesham. This estate occupies the site of the Battle of Evesham at which Simon de Montfort was killed by a Royalist soldier and his body brutally mutilated.

The walk took us up Greenhill where, on the left of the road, just past the Greenhill Preparatory School, was a pond known as Battle Well. We stopped to watch some frogs swimming in the pond, although we did not know it at the time this pond was used to water the horses of Simon de Montfort's troops during the battle of Evesham.

At the rear of the pond a derelict two-storied house with no roof stood in a small copse. This was an open invitation to two young boys to explore. The wooden staircase was intact but somewhat rickety; there were no floor boards upstairs so we had to walk along the joists, adding a spice of danger as we looked out of glassless windows. Eventually we tired of the game and Eric made his way downstairs before me. I followed a minute or so later as I was further from the staircase and had to negotiate more joists. The stairs were well lit by the early afternoon sun shining through the roofless house. As I went down, a dark shadowy figure passed me against the inner wall, moving up the stairs. Although it was a hot day I felt an icy cold chill in the air. I made my way down as fast as possible. I wish to point out that at that time I knew nothing of the history of the Battle Well and there was therefore no auto-suggestion to account for my experience.

In the mid 1930's the derelict house was replaced by two beautiful big houses built on the Battle Well site. One was occupied by F C Byrd who owned a confectionery and bakery business in Bridge Street.

Alone in the almonry

Most of my boyhood and early youth was spent in the lovely old house known as The Almonry, now the Almonry Museum which is situated on Merstow Green at the end of Vine Street. It was then a private residence, the home of my family where I lived happily with my father, mother, two brothers and a sister. I loved the old house dearly and still do to this day.

The Almonry was that part of the Benedictine Abbey of Evesham which housed the Brother Monk known as the Almoner whose duty it was to help the poor and needy.

The Abbey dates originally from about AD 702 and was founded by St Egwin, Bishop of Worcester, who was the first Abbot. The earliest reference to an Almoner occurs in AD 1214. In 1538 Henry VIII ordered the dissolution of the Abbey, but for some reason the Bell Tower, the Churches of St Laurence and All Saints and the Almonry were spared. King Henry leased the Almonry to the last Abbot for his lifetime and in 1545 ownership was granted to Philip Hoby who had acquired most of the remains of the Abbey.

The stonework of the Almonry is that part of the original building but additions in wattle and daub were made by the Tudors in 1540, and much later in 1800 other additions were made.

Most of the "ghostly happenings" took place when I was alone in the house. I would say that perhaps I was an over-confident young man, as I was quite unafraid, being physically very fit and feeling indestructible and able to cope with anything, and in any case I felt that the house was a friendly place and not at all awesome.

For whom the bell tolls

When I lived in the Almonry, there were electric bell pushes in the sitting room, dining room and four of the bedrooms, with an indicator board in the kitchen.

On numerous occasions, during the day and night, one particular bell would ring from the main front bedroom next to the oak panelled room. On going to investigate we always found the bell button pushed in and had some difficulty in releasing it. No matter how hard I tried I could never get the button to remain in the pushed-in position. It would always spring back to the ready-to-push position as it should do. An electrician checked the wiring for a short but found nothing. He changed the bell push and even so the bell still rang from time to time for no apparent reason. There appeared to be no reason why it should only happen in that particular room.

Open sesame

I had my supper in the dining room and was walking down the long stone corridor to take my tray back to the kitchen. At the end of this particular corridor a beautiful stone lantern is supported some two feet above the stone paving against the wall of the main cellar which was at one time used as a jail, contemporary with the stocks which are at the front of the house. The lantern is about four feet six inches in height and has a small oak door about two feet long by a foot wide which can be opened to look into the cellar. This small hatch was used to pass food to the inmates of the jail. A very heavy oak door beside the lantern opens on to the top of a short flight of stone steps which lead into the largest of the three cellars. This door is beside the lantern.

As I was walking down the corridor the small door in the lantern opened wide and remained open for at least ten seconds. I watched in amazement because it was a very still summer evening with not a breath of wind and even on windy days the lantern door has never opened of its own volition. After about ten seconds the door slammed shut with a bang as if had been closed by someone in a temper. After taking my tray to the kitchen I opened the door to the cellar and walked down the few stone steps leading to the first and largest cellar. As I went down the steps I felt an icy coldness. Neither of the three cellars felt cold as I searched them for an intruder, without success. On remounting the steps to leave the cellars I again experienced the same icy coldness.

The almonry apparition

Usually I went to bed at about 10 pm and never woke until 7 am, in fact my family teased me that I could sleep through canon fire. This, however, was not the case one beautiful summer night in 1938. Quite out of character I woke up suddenly with no feeling of having been asleep. I was wide awake when the Bell Tower clock struck 2 am. My bed ran alongside a low leaded diamond paned lattice window which I had opened wide before going to bed to let in the fragrant scent of the white jasmine and honeysuckle which grew directly beneath my window. Without having to get out of bed I could look directly into the garden. It was a bright moonlit night with a full moon and everything in the garden was as clear as day. As I looked I saw a dark figure very slowly moving across the lawn from the direction of the old quince tree, which sadly has been uprooted to make space for a shelter to house the agricultural implements for the museum.

My room had once been the granary of the Almoner and could be reached via the main bedroom at the rear of the house through a cupboard-like space, where subsequently a trap door had been made in the floor to expose the Priest's Hiding Hole that had been discovered there. Two stairs then led up to a beautiful heavy oak door which opened on to my room. Across the room opposite the window beside my bed, was a low square door through which the sacks of grain were loaded into the room and wooden steps led down from this door to the cobbled courtyard beside the old stone cross in the garden.

To return to the figure on the lawn, I quickly put on my slippers and using the outside steps gained access to the garden. This probably took less than fifteen seconds. The figure was still walking very slowly in the direction of the summerhouse and shrubbery. Believing it to be an intruder who had climbed over the high garden wall, I walked quickly towards him. I could now see more clearly the figure of a man, dressed in a garment of dark material like a monk's habit. The man's head was covered by a cowl which was part of the garment and I could clearly see his hands and feet which appeared white. There may have been sandals on the feet but I was unable to make them out. The position of his hands were as if he was holding a book or some object, and his head was bowed as if looking at the object or reading. By this time, everything having taken probably less than a minute, I was quite near the figure. I shouted, "Hey, what are you doing here?". By that time he had reached the summerhouse where the shrubbery cast dark shadows. In spite of my call to him he never increased his slow pace and when I was no more than four feet away he suddenly disappeared. I searched the shrubbery and all round the summerhouse but could not find him. I knew no-one had climbed over the wall to the Abbey Road as I had a clear and unrestricted view of the entire wall in that area. I could only therefore assume I had seen the ghost of a monk. The loose-fitting habit made it impossible to tell if he was of a slim or heavy build, but he was shorter than I am, I would say about five feet eight inches. I did not experience any drop in temperature, even when I was only about four feet away from him. I had intended to reach out to touch him but he must have sensed my intention for at that moment he simply disappeared.

In my last Will and Testament I have requested that I be cremated and my ashes strewn in the garden near the summerhouse where I used to sit for hours on end, happy just to look at the beautiful house and garden which I love so much. I knew how lucky and privileged I was to live there for at least some of my life.

Maybe my ghost will be able to keep company with the monk I saw in the garden.

Uncle's footsteps

Many ghost stories have a historic value in that they preserve the thoughts, feelings and day-to-day life of the characters involved in a way that the history books, which must concentrate on facts, cannot hope to emulate. The next two anecdotes are not only a ghost stories but facets of social history. The first is by Alys Whiting who still lives in Evesham.

During the 1920's our family lived at 1, The Leys. In those days there was no gas or electricity and the house was lit by those paraffin lamps with a long chimney. There were no luxuries such as stair carpet – we had wooden stairs and at the top was a tiny fireplace with a small stone slab set into the floor in front. This slab was in two halves which made a clonking noise as you walked over them.

One Sunday morning, my younger sister and I were watching my mother clean the chimney of one of these lamps. She was sitting at a table with a yellow duster in her hand, breathing on the duster then polishing the glass, when we herd the stone upstairs go 'clonk'! The three of us sat up and listened, then we heard these heavy, hob-nailed boots coming slowly down the stairs.

We were terrified. We rushed to the front door and went out into the street. My father was a carter and worked for Mr Stewart who lived in a large house just round the corner. (I often used to help him with the horses and he used to let me lead some of the gentle shires into the meadow at the end of the day). The three of us went along to the yard where the drays were kept and told one of the men there that we thought that someone had broke into the house. This man got a big stick and said, 'I'll soon sort them out' and went back to the house with us. He went upstairs but came down saying, 'There isn't anybody!'

We went back into the house then, and about half-an-hour later a knock came at the back door and an older boy was standing there saying, 'Can I have a word with you, please?' He told us that my father's brother had been found with his throat cut at Littleton. He must have died just about the time that we heard his footsteps.

I don't know why his footsteps should be heard in our house – if they were his footsteps. I can only say that he was our favourite uncle and he spent a lot of time at our house.

Ghost on the loo[†]

Mrs Shovelton was born in July 1923 and has now retired to Malvern, but this incident occurred when she lived in Port Street, Evesham.

When I was eleven years of age we lived in an old house with only an outside loo which was situated along a yard at the back of the building.

One afternoon on returning from school I followed my usual habit and rushed straight to the loo… and froze on the spot. Seated there was an old man with a long white beard, a black skull cap, black cloak and holding a black walking cane. It seemed an eternity before I could avert my gaze, move my leaden legs and rush indoors screaming, 'Mum, there's an old man sitting on our loo!'. Mum told me not to be stupid, took my hand and marched me along to the back of the house. Of course, no-one was there.

When I had stopped shaking Mum asked me to describe this man and when I had done so she gave me threepence to spend and made no further comment.

That night when I went to bed I could not get to sleep and later, when my parents came up to bed, I heard Mum say to Dad, 'Our kid described old Johny Hopkins as the man sitting on the loo'. John Hopkins had been a bell ringer at the local church but had died more than four years before I had my vision…

†First submitted to BBC Hereford & Worcester for their ghost story competition.

Look mummy!

For a contemporary tale of Evesham ghosts we look at a young professional couple, Derek and Angela Adams*, with a small son who, in 1994, moved into one of the older-type houses in the suburbs. This is one of those strange occasions when building work on a house seems to activate paranormal phenomena. Derek gives his version of events first.

When we moved here the house had been occupied by an elderly lady. We've asked her about the strange happenings and she says that nothing of that kind occurred while she was here. When we moved in we started major restructural work; one of my first jobs was to get rid of the downstairs loo which led off the kitchen. We seem to have started a touch paper and all hell broke loose. For example, we were sitting in the front room one evening when the light started flashing, then the bulb popped right out of the standard lamp. It didn't fall on the floor but just lay on the lamp holder.

The paranormal activity seemed to stop when I finished the one lot of structural work but it started again when we had central heating put in. I explained to the workmen that we thought the house was haunted and they took it with a pinch of salt. Then one of the workman unplugged the telephone, wound the cord round it and put it on the bed. A few minutes later the telephone started ringing. The workman said he left the room as quickly as he could.

In the bathroom we have a small strip light above the sink mirror. One night, a few weeks after we had moved in, I switched off this light and turned to leave the bathroom. My wife was in the bedroom making the bed with the door open and the light on, so that I could see quite clearly. At that point I saw the shape of a man in front of me. I thought it was a friend who was staying with us for a few days, so I said, 'Goodnight' to him but there was no reply. I thought, 'Miserable thing'. However, when I turned the corner, who should I see coming down the attic stairs but my friend! I must have gone pale and ashen because when I went into the bedroom, my wife said, 'What's the matter?'. I told her I thought I had just seen a ghost!

Angela now takes up the story.

I always know when the ghost is going to be active because the dog gets twitchy. He stands at the door of the kitchen, looking up at something and growling. Then I know my three-year old son is going to see it a lot, he sees it more than anyone. He sits in his bedroom playing and he says that he is playing with an old gentleman. One day, we were sitting one each side of him in the bedroom and he called out, 'Come in, come in, come and play with me.' We said to him, 'Who are you talking to?' and he said, 'That man over there!' At another time my son went to the bottom of the stairs and said, 'Look mummy, there's a man coming down the stairs'.

I'm very pregnant and I get up at all hours. One night I was staggering to the toilet and I fell over. Someone touched my elbow, holding it just like an elderly man does when he's escorting you. I thought at first that I had brushed against something and I quickly looked around but there was nothing nearby. Afterwards I thought, 'Hang on, that was nothing like an accidental brush!'. When I went back to bed I told my husband I'd been 'touched' and we had a look at my elbow. There were red fingermarks on it.

We asked two Spiritualists to visit the house. They said that the entity didn't understand why other people have moved into his house and were using his things. They said that they thought his name was Jack or James Williams. We thought this was a bit OTT at the time – they had asked us so many questions they could easily have come up with a name – but a couple of weeks later a load of papers arrived about the history of the house and there, smack in the middle was a death certificate, dated 1834, for John Williams.

It bothers me that the ghost is a man. I wouldn't mind so much if it was a female ghost. My mother-in-law says that, if I feel uncomfortable about it, I should tell it to go away. I do this and it does seem to go away for a while.

When the ghost is about I can smell this strange smell, the kind you get in old houses, but after the spiritualists had visited there was a flowery smell, it was really lovely. It lasted for quite a few days then it faded.

KIDDERMINSTER

NTIL RECENT YEARS, Kidderminster claimed to be 'the carpet metropolis of the world'. The town developed on the banks of the river Stour, whose waters were said to have special properties which gave 'brilliancy and durableness' to the colours. The first carpets were made as far back as the early 1600s and were highly-prized table or wall hangings. Like needle-making, this was at first a cottage industry, then the first carpet works were established in 1735 south of Mill Street. In the 1860's, the Earl of Dudley built a series of weaving sheds for hire in the Green Street and New Street area, with steam power available.

The Victorian mills have given Kidderminster a reputation of being an unlovely town, but as time mellows the red brick and distances us from the horrors of working in them, they acquire a character and a charm of their own.

In addition to carpets, Kidderminster produced Rowland Hill, who introduced the postal service as we know it today, with payment for delivery of the letter being made by a stamp. The Postmaster General of that time commented, 'Of all the wild and visionary schemes which I have ever heard of this is the most extraordinary'. Despite this it received Royal Assent in 1839. Rowland Hill was born in Blackwell Street in 1795 and the telephone exchange was built on the site of his house. The present building dates back to 1939, when a new exchange was opened.

Some of the local people were in the Auxiliary Fire Service during the war and they can remember fire watching from the top of the exchange. They say that rumours about a haunting were in circulation then and the men used to enjoy elaborating on the tales to frighten those of a nervous disposition. (See newspaper cutting, page 43).

However, there is one man who has first hand knowledge of the ghost and who can tell his experiences exactly as they occurred..

A ghost on the line

Ronald Griffin

In May 1969 I was transferred to Kidderminster Telephone Exchange from redundant civil service posts with the Royal Army Pay Corps and RAF. I received six weeks training and became a Night Telephonist at the exchange, remaining there until further redundancies in 1976.

My most sensational and memorable experience on nights was the haunting of a ghost. Lifts started to go up and down without being called. Pencils disappeared into thin air. Doors would open and shut during the early hours and I often saw a black shadow wandering around the room. Although from time to time others had witnessed strange happenings, the friendly ghost mostly appeared when I was on duty. I frequently heard doors creak and one night, during my break in the rest room, I felt cold and the blanket covering me was whisked away.

It was three o'clock in the morning when the buzzer called me to the board, I answered with the usual 'Number please'; a strange husky voice on the line called, 'Hello – hello!' followed by amused laughter as it faded away. I then felt an icy shiver run through me as I recognised the sound of the selectors from the engineers' exchange below. No-one was on duty, but it was from down there that I received the call.

Another time I was about to report a fault, when my pencil was snatched out of my hand, never to be found.

This was in December 1975 and the story of the ghost got to the local press. I gave them an interview and told them of my experiences with the apparition. This resulted in a photograph of me taken at the board, with headlines on the front page: 'Has the ghost of Rowland Hill come back to haunt the Post Office's exchange'. The article culminated in my giving further interviews to the national press and the National Enquirer of America. They sent a photographer down from Manchester and he took about eighty shots, mostly of myself on the switchboard surrounded by lighted candles. All very dramatic and exciting although the ghost, shyly, didn't appear for them.

However, the ghost did finally make himself known to me through automatic writing. I was sitting alone at my desk with a pencil in my hand. (2 am). I was about to write something, when the pencil started to move forming large scrawly words. The words spelt out the young man's name, then went on to write a few lines saying that he had fallen from a girder and had been killed.

This was proved some months later when a Kidderminster man read about the ghost in a Post Office Journal. He said that he was certain it was a builder killed in a fall when the Telephone Exchange was being built in the early 1930's.

Today Kidderminster is an Operation Exchange no more. The switchboards and a network of communications lasting 60 years has gone for ever and, most likely, the ghost with it.

The night staff at the GPO's switchboard in Kidderminster are waiting in trepidation for August 27. This is the date of the 100th anniversary of Sir Rowland Hill's death, and perhaps the date when his ghost will embark on a special spook to mark the occasion.

The ghost of Sir Rowland Hill is said to haunt the GPO's centre in Waterloo Street , as this building is on the site of his birthplace. Several of the night staff have experienced strange happenings over the years. Mr Percy Wright, who has been with the GPO for 30 years, says that he can often feel the presence of the ghost. "sometimes it's as though he's right by you." he said.

"On one occasion I was sitting down in the early hours of the morning when the bar on a fire escape door at the rear of the building rose up and the doors slowly opened," said Mr Wright. "I was amazed as it was a perfectly still night and there was no rational explanation for the incident."

On another occasion Mr T.T. Davies, also on night duty, was resting in the lounge one night when he saw an outline of a ghostly figure drift past him Like Mr Wright he was not a great believer in ghosts, but this incident certainly shook him up.

Other mysterious incidents have happened, doors and windows opening for no apparent reason, a blue haze of smoke drifting across the switchboard, and ghostly phone calls being made inside the building.

One queer thing about this ghost is that he has never haunted any of the women staff, but perhaps that is because women were not employed in the Post Office in Rowland Hill's time.

Worcester Evening News, Wyre edition, 17th August 1979.

The malevolent spirit

One of the first questions usually asked about ghosts is – 'Can they hurt you?'.The number of incidents where ghosts have caused some kind of injury is extremely small. Where a house has a poltergeist, it is not unknown for someone to be hit by an object, but usually this is tiny, such as a biro. However, it has been known, very occasionally, for an apparition to leave a mark or a bruise.The following story by Bill Perkins* is one of the very few cases of an apparently malevolent entity.

My late uncle was born and reared in a mining village in South Wales. He worked in the pits and as a young athletic man was forced by the depression to come to Kidderminster to look for work in the early 1930's. Here he met and married my mother's youngest sister and lived in the family home in Franchise Street. The house is an ordinary two-bedroomed terraced house built about 1880.

Sometime in the late 1930s he, for some unknown reason, was sleeping in the attic. One night he woke up with the distinct impression that somebody was trying to strangle him. He lit a candle and looked round but no-one else was in the room.

Some years later, on a visit to his relations in South Wales, his brother told him of the same thing happening to him in the same attic and the same bed on the one and only occasion that he came up to Kidderminster.

Both the two men involved were down-to-earth ex-miners with no vivid imagination. However, I helped to empty the house when my uncle moved to an old people's bungalow and I did not encounter anything out of the ordinary.

LEOMINSTER (Herefordshire)

HE ANCIENT TOWN OF LEOMINSTER grew around a monastery or priory founded by a Mercian king in the 7th century. There is a reference to Leominster in the Bayeaux tapestry. Before Leominster Priory was built a convent stood on the site, and the Abbess was carried off and raped by Swaine, the brother of King Harold. Soon afterwards Harold was, of course, killed in the battle of Hastings of 1066, and William Rufus became king.

A great and famous school of architecture and sculpture, the Herefordshire School, was based at Leominster during the twelfth century. One piece of their work which has survived almost intact is Kilpeck Church but other remnants can be found throughout the Midlands. At Leominster Priory, the capitals of the south door and the small stone carving on the inside west wall is the work of the Herefordshire School.

The very old and the very young

Little May lives with her parents and younger brother on the northern edge of the town. Some children are said to be wise before their time and May is one of them. A solemn, sensible two year old, she has an extraordinary vocabulary and chatters away as if she has just been released from solitary confinement. However, in March 1996, this pretty, curly-haired little girl unwittingly caused her parents such anxiety that they felt obliged to ask a local paranormal society for help. Her father explains:

> We keep having these surges of electricity when the lights suddenly increase for a few seconds. When this happens May just freaks out and she screams the house down. We can't stop her. We haven't lived in this house all that long – we moved in about six months ago and it started almost from the minute that we arrived.
>
> About two weeks after we moved here, when we were still living out of boxes in the kitchen, May pointed to the back kitchen door and said there was a man there. We had a look and we could see no sign of anyone. At first, we thought it was an imaginary friend but then, as time went on, we realised that she only sees him in the kitchen. This happens most often when she's having breakfast – suddenly, she will start chattering away. We ask her who she is talking to and she says that she can see a man sitting by the door. We have tried to find out all we can about this person. We ask her,

'What's he doing?' and she tells us that he's drinking juice. We ask, 'Is it orange juice?' and she says, 'No, it's Nan's juice'. This would be a pint of beer! Sometimes she says, 'Man – railway' so we assume he's associated with the railway which runs quite close to the bottom of our garden.

She won't go into the kitchen unless we are in there with her. The kitchen here is exactly the same as the one in our old house and she was going into it quite readily there. We have spoken to the woman who lived in the house before us and she told us that her two young children were terrified of men and she could never understand why.

Something else we have noticed is that May usually sees this man when she and I are alone together. My wife usually has to get up to the baby several times each night so she tends to sleep late in the morning. I give May her breakfast and we are alone in the kitchen. The surge of electricity which terrifies May usually occurs at about 7.30 in the evening, when I'm putting her to bed.

We have other strange things happening as well. We have trouble with electrical appliances and I seem to have the knack of short-circuiting things. Sometimes, at the bottom of the stairs is a cold patch, there's no reason for it and we have noticed that the cat will never go through this cold patch, she always walks round it. Articles disappear then turn up later where you looked in the first place, it happens so often that we have started keeping a list of all our missing articles with the date. This happened in our previous house and it seems to have followed us.

As I go round the corner of the house I feel what I can only describe as a panic attack and I avoid looking out of the upstairs window because I feel that I am going to see something disagreeable. I wondered if anything unpleasant has ever happened here, on the northern tip of the town. The house is new, it was only built in 1991 on farmland, but local people tell me that this area was the original site of Leominster and was known as 'the marshes', then about 1200 it moved south to the other side of the river to be under the protection of the monastery.

I have been down to Leominster library and although the librarian was unable to confirm this he did give me one interesting piece of news. A nunnery stood on the site of Leominster Priory until 1046 and the little village church was elsewhere. Local tradition has it that this stood where my house is now.

Does this in any way explain the surges of electricity and May's screams? We don't mind her talking to an invisible man, this keeps her happy all through breakfast time, but her screams are more than anyone can stand.

The monk and the Talbot Hotel

Wool and woollen cloths were England's most important exports in the middle ages and Leominster was a local centre of the wool trade until it died out early in the 19th century.

The town therefore has many fine old houses, among them The Talbot Hotel in West Street which consists of three houses, the first Georgian, the second early Georgian and the third an earlier, timber-framed house. Robert Creswell is the manager and he has an interesting tale to tell.

The Talbot Hotel

Tradition has it that the Talbot Hotel is named after a dog of that breed. In the days of highwaymen, the dog used to run alongside the coaches and once when a coach was attacked, he managed to distract the highwayman so that the coach got away. The original coaching house was quite small and the present hotel and restaurant is the result of several buildings being linked together. On one of the landings, you can see the gable ends of the house next door, and we have another section which, by all accounts, was a cottage and served as quarters for the stage coach drivers.

One evening in about 1990, after a number of long and tiring events over several days, I left the hotel in the capable hands of my assistant manager and treated myself to a night off. Up the stairs I went for a sleep in a particular room which is in the centre of the hotel, and overlooks a central service well and flat roof area of the building. At about one o'clock in the morning I was to all intents asleep, when I was awoken by a pressure on the lower part of my legs. I stirred and to my amazement I saw that there appeared to be a monk hopping about on my bed. I did not have his full weight on my legs but it was just sufficient to wake me up. The apparition was very clear, I could see that he was wearing a dark grey habit and was about 35 or 40 years of age with a grin from ear to ear. As I awoke I drew myself up on the bed from a flat position. With that, the monk jumped off the bed onto the floor to my left and started to dance and jig around. His knees were going up in the air and he was tittering, 'He, he he!'. I thought, 'What's going on here?' To my right was a window and on the wall was a mirror and I told myself that it must be a reflection in either of these of something that was going on outside, but no, I could see that was not so. In any case, there was no light anywhere so it could not have been a reflection. I reached out to the side of the bed and switched on the table lamp at which the apparition disappeared.

I was rather taken aback by this episode but I hoped that it was going to happen again so that I could question him to see if he could be linked to a historical event or anything in the records.

I came down and told everyone the next morning and they all had a good laugh. I was accused of being in an alcoholic haze but I protested that I had only had two beers!

One morning a few months later I was in reception when a guest came in who had been staying in the room next to the one in which I had seen the monk. He asked – it was quite impromptu – 'Has this place got a ghost?'. I said that I thought it had, and he replied, 'I have seen it!' and he started to describe the apparition exactly as I had experienced it. I have since heard that other people have seen it too.

The Talbot Hotel is situated on the cross roads in the centre of Leominster, the cross roads are known as 'The Iron Cross' and is still referred to as this by the older residents of the town. This is where, in the time of the religious persecutions, any priests who had come to light were hung, drawn and quartered. There were rich pickings for the Protestants in this part of Herefordshire, many illegal religious orders were living hereabouts as the ground was fenland and marshland, no-one wanted it and so there was plenty of room for them to go into hiding. Sentences were carried out by the local butcher. The story goes that when the butcher came to execute a certain monk by the name of Cadwallader he made a mess of it so that the death was not quick. It is said that the monk still haunts these parts. Was it Cadwallader that I saw on my bed?

The man who caught a ghost

From the windows of Frank Marsden's house he can see the tower of Leominster Priory rising above the rooftops. He has been interested in the paranormal ever since he experienced a curious phenomenon in his early teens.

A few years ago, Frank was approached by an elderly country couple, Ernest★ and Amy★ who had heard that he was very knowledgeable about the paranormal and wanted his help. They were experiencing strange manifestations in their home which were frightening the wife's mother, who was living with them at that time. They needed someone whose confidentiality they could trust as they had lived for many years in an old rented cottage and did not wish to draw attention to themselves by letting it become known that they were having these problems.

Frank takes up the story.

Ernest told me that the manifestation first began with footsteps overhead in the roof area. At first, he put this down to rats and thought nothing of it but after he had put down enough rat poison 'to exterminate all the rats in Herefordshire' and the footsteps continued, he realised that he had to look elsewhere for the cause.

He sometimes had the feeling that anther family was living in the house with them. He regularly heard the noise of a coalskuttle being filled and breakfast being laid in the kitchen.

Curious incidents occurred. Amy's mother had two sons and a photograph of one of them stood on her dressing table. One night, the photograph disappeared and reappeared in another room on Ernest's bedside table.

In the living room downstairs, some verses by Patience Strong stood on the mantelpiece. These were mysteriously removed from the frame and dropped on the floor next to the electric fire.

Articles went missing and were found in places where no-one could have put them. Ernest's pension book disappeared and reappeared in a small cupboard at ceiling level which was disused and kept shut. He also had a large, heavy ring which was spirited away, then when Amy was dusting, she heard a nearby vase rattling of its own accord, looked in and there was the ring.

Amy came downstairs three mornings in succession to find a bizarre manifestation had taken place during the night. The first time, she found three saucepans in a line on the carpet, on the second morning these had been replaced by three books and on the third morning, three packets of cornflakes were in a row – all had been opened but none had been spilt.

Footsteps could be heard walking up and down the stairs and in the bed-rooms overhead. There were other noises too, and one of these was very startling, it sounded like a shotgun going off in the room. Amy's mother told me that one Sunday morning, a man had called with his young son to see Ernest who happened to be out. The mother had entertained them in their snug little sitting room while they waited for him to return. The three of them were sitting, there, peacefully chatting, when suddenly, the sound of a shotgun went off in the room and a spiral of smoke appeared from the carpet, followed by a blue, electric-type ball of lightning which floated across the room. The visitor and his son made a hasty exit.

My first ever visit to the cottage was on a rainy evening in October 1981. Amy was upstairs decorating a room with a family friend and as I walked in through the front door she called, 'I'm glad you've come, the noises have started!' and the two women hurried downstairs. I ran upstairs and heard noises coming from a low cupboard. They sounded as if they were being made by a large and heavy animal – as if a couple of cats had been shut in there. I opened the cupboard and found it crammed full of picture frames. There was no way that a mouse could have got in there, let alone a cat!

I stood and waited to hear if anything else happened. Sure enough, after a few minutes, heavy footsteps came up the stairs. The door of the room in which I was standing slowly opened and I expected to see Ernest, but no-one was there. The footsteps clearly and distinctly walked across the bedroom and stopped in front of the dressing table.

Again, I waited, hoping to see some physical manifestation. I became aware that in one of the darker corners of the room I could see a cluster of dozens of blue sparks – the cluster was about a foot in diameter. I watched while it faded away, then I waited for a few minutes longer and as nothing else occurred I went downstairs.

As soon as I rejoined the others the walls began to vibrate with a noise as if a wardrobe upstairs was being dragged loudly across the floor.

Some of these manifestations seemed mindless but other occurrences, such as placing saucepans and books in a row, appeared to be the work of some intelligence so I devised a test. I ranged a set of dominoes in numer-ical order on the dressing table where the footsteps had stopped on my first evening and left instructions to Ernest and Amy that they were not to be touched. A few days later I returned and thought at first that they were still as I left them, then I noticed that the three and the seven had been transposed.

I made enquiries to find out who had lived in the house beforehand. I managed to contact the previous owner, a reclusive character who had lived there alone. On asking if he had heard strange noises, he replied that he had, but had put it down to rats.

Over the next few years, the manifestations continued. One strange sound which occurred many times and which I myself heard, came from the roof and sounded as if a pebble were being thrown on the roof then rolling down the tiles. Curiously, the sound trace was exactly the same each time.

One Sunday afternoon when Ernest and Amy were out and Amy's mother was sitting with a friend, they were in the living room, the one knitting, the other just sitting, when suddenly, a decorated chrome-traced teapot (which was an ornament and not used) levitated from the sideboard, described an arc and deposited itself on the carpet in front of them. Amy entered this incident in a competition asking for ghost stories and was pleased to see her letter published.

Even Ernest, normally an unemotional type of person, was unnerved one morning in November 1992. He was sitting in the kitchen when a five inch pot, complete with compost and plant, removed itself from the window sill, flew through the air and hit him on the thigh. Amy was in the next room and Ernest shouted to her, 'Did you see that plant pot!' to which Amy shouted back that things were also happening round her. She had been sitting near a pile of books when, suddenly, books had removed themselves from the bottom of the pile and flung themselves across the room.

A few days later, Amy retired to bed earlier than usual with a headache, and Ernest was watching television. They had had a mild disagreement over the television volume. At about halfpast ten, Amy was tossing and turning, trying to get to sleep when, to her annoyance, the television was turned up full blast. She heard the dialogue of a play and some music which continued until 11.15. She assumed that Ernest had gone to bed and turned on the television in his bedroom next door. When she confronted him he stared at her, open-mouthed. He had gone to bed shortly after Amy and had certainly not switched on the television in his bedroom – it was temporarily out of use as the aerial had been disconnected.

At 7 am on Friday, 11 December 1992 there occurred a manifestation which broke new ground. At this time, Ernest was alone in the house save for his dog, a Lurcher, which was with him in his bedroom. The dog began to act in an agitated manner and then started to whine. Immediately, Ernest suspected intruders downstairs, despite the house having been made secure with all doors and windows locked. Anticipating a confrontation with burglars and having shotgun to hand, he was seriously considering loading two cartridges when next he heard footfalls on the stairs. These slowly ascended, moved across the landing and came to a stop outside his bedroom door. Ernest froze, in a state of intense shock, as a ghostly humanoid form passed through the closed door and proceeded to the foot of the bed, before slowly dissolving into thin air. The entity was not sufficiently materialised to enable determination of features or clothing but its height was about five and a half feet.

Following the 'flying plant pot' incident, I, too, experienced a similar phenomenon in my kitchen. An identical (five inch) plant pot, containing plant and compost, was dashed to the kitchen floor while I was sitting in the adjacent living room. There was no-one else in the house other than the cat, which was with me on the settee. I should point out that Ernest's plant pot was a gift from me the previous Christmas.

Noises of an unmistakable paranormal origin began to occur quite frequently in my house, such as strange thuds and bangs coming from the cooker and continuing for several minutes. These were not dissimilar to the noises which I had heard coming from Ernest and Amy's upstairs' cupboard on my first visit. When I was in my bedroom I heard footsteps downstairs and as I ran down the stairs to investigate, the walls vibrated and the whole house shook. A few days later I came downstairs one morning to find that a lampshade, which I am sure was quite secure, had overnight fallen to the floor and smashed. Another morning, I discovered that the whole of the ceiling in the hallway had fallen down. My house is fairly modern and should not be subject to this kind of dilapidation.

Probably the most dramatic of my own phenomena was to experience a shotgun blast a few feet behind me when in my bedroom. It was 7.20 in the morning and again, I was alone in the house. I had secretly felt somewhat sceptical of Ernest's account, where he compared an unexplained sound to a shotgun being fired. I can now affirm the accuracy of his comparison. For a few seconds, I felt deafened. Later that day I met Ernest and he told me that at exactly the same time in his house, the same noise had occurred.

It is interesting to note an apparent significant connection between events happening at the cottage and those subsequently occurring at my own house, and it is tempting to believe that some ghostly agent has migrated from the 'haunted cottage'.

Before concluding, Amy has asked me to mention that they had some strange happenings in their previous house, going back to the 1960's. This was also an old cottage on the outskirts of Leominster. There, Amy frequently saw the ghost of an old woman wearing a white frilled bonnet and black buttoned shoes. She sat and rocked in a rocking chair which belonged to Ernest's family. When they vacated this cottage and moved to the present dwelling they took the rocking chair which would often be witnessed rocking by itself – the ghostly woman not being visible. This so unnerved the family that Ernest eventually put the chair to the flames. The former cottage was eventually demolished when human bones were found.

In conclusion, for my part I have done all I possibly could to gain an understanding of these phenomena in an attempt to gain some degree of control. They continue unabated and still as enigmatic as ever. As with the Loch Ness monster, it is perhaps as well that they remain shrouded in mystery; therein lies their attraction.

PERSHORE

HE YEAR WAS 1944 and the beautiful old priory in Pershore town centre lay shrouded in darkness in the early hours of morning. Suddenly, the air of this quiet market town was filled with loud screams coming from the priory grounds. Local residents awoke and listened. A few living near the centre dressed hastily and rushed out to investigate, but no culprit was ever found. This happened not once, but on a succession of nights, and the phenomenon was so extraordinary that in a time when the progress of the war was of prime interest, it found its way into the national press. The screams ended as suddenly as they began and the source was never discovered.

Pershore Abbey

Pershore's colourful origins must have filled the town with strange entities. The town was built to serve the abbey, founded as early as 690, and although the abbey has been rebuilt several times, most of the surviving remnant goes back to the eleventh century. About a thousand years ago the monastery was owned by Duke Alphere 'who did great injury to the domestic establishments of the diocese'. After a life of crime, he met with a horrible death, 'being eaten of vermin'. His son, Odda, 'restored what his father had plundered' and vowed to remain celibate lest a son of his should follow in the family footsteps. Odda became monk at Deerhurst and was later Earl of Devonshire, Somerset, Dorset and Cornwall. He died in 1056 and is buried at Pershore.

Today, many towns survive on the tourist industry and it was much the same with religious houses in early medieval days. Their wealth was achieved by attracting pilgrims. One of the daughters of Alfred the Great (of burnt cakes fame), had entered a convent at Winchester and was later appointed Abbess of Pershore. She was buried at Winchester and miracles began to be performed at her tomb. Odda therefore arranged to purchase a few of her bones for Pershore Abbey. However, the bones which were sent were evidently those which 'worked', because miracles started happening at Pershore whereas they died out at Winchester. After some bureaucratic wrangling, the bones were eventually returned to Winchester and then, probably towards the end of the nineteenth century, they were returned to Pershore. Of course, by then the bones had no value and the Abbey didn't know what to do with them. In 1890, the chancel at Yardley, which was in the same diocese, was being lengthened and so these once-priceless relics were ignominiously buried under the floor there.

George and the dragon

Another strange story comes from Mrs Bryant in Drakes Broughton, a rapidly expanding rural community on the A44, just north of Pershore.

Our family moved into a council house there in the early 1970's when my older sister was twenty, my younger sister was four and I was eleven. The house had been built in 1945 by the side of an old bridleway which was narrow, twisting and gloomy. Local people said that it had been a favourite haunt of highway men who, whenever they were caught, were hung from the surrounding trees.

My parents used to have the most dreadful arguments about switching off radios and rings on cookers. Mum was always certain that she had switched them off but dad would find them on again. I also remember their rows about the front door. Dad used to swear that he locked it at night before he went to bed but mum used to come down in the morning and find it wide open. Other strange things happened, the fuses blew quite regularly and clothes were thrown about. When we returned from holiday my parents put their cases in their bedroom while they sorted themselves out and when they went to unpack, their clothes had been thrown all round the bedroom.

My parents had to call the plumber in because the immersion heater at the top of the stairs was leaking badly. The plumber said that someone had undone all the nuts and bolts on the immersion and my parents said it must be one of the children larking about. The plumber said that no child could have undone them, they needed a monkey wrench and a great deal of masculine strength.

Ever since we moved into the house my younger sister had been asking why my father kept waking her up at night, which led my mother to suspect that the house was haunted. She assumed it was some kind of entity and called it 'George'.

We all seemed to suffer from George. My younger sister was ill with asthma for the three years that we lived there. My mother and older sister were hassled by George more and more frequently so that towards the end of our three years there, they felt or heard him every day. They heard the tapping and footsteps, and every night they were pulled down the bed by their ankles. Occasionally they saw him, he appeared in three ways, as a solid black shape, as a solid silver shape, or half and half – the top half black and the bottom half silver. They complained so much that the press heard about it and came to interview them.

As for me, I was sick every night that we lived in that house. I felt as if someone were putting their fingers down my throat. I only saw George once and that was in October 1971. I was sitting up in bed, I looked up and there he was. He was a very big man, tall and broad – and filled the whole doorway. He was slightly elevated and appeared to float, but I could only see him down to his knees, after that he was missing so that his knees were two or three feet off the ground. He was very much silhouetted so that he was just solid, dark, charcoal grey, although I could make out that his beard and moustache had streaks of grey and he had white tufts poking out round his hands. I have a history book with a picture of a Cavalier and he looked like that, with a big rimmed hat and a loose cloak, made from coarse fabric but possibly with a hood. He was just standing there with his hands clasped in front of his tummy button.

That was the only time I actually saw him although he shook me awake several times and I once felt him hold my hand. My mother suggested that I should drew a sketch of him which I did in an old notebook, then I grabbed a knitting needle and stabbed holes in the drawing. The next day the notebook had disappeared and has never been found since.

However, he seemed to take my personality over so that I became quite aggressive and was really nasty to my parents. I knew that my behaviour was not acceptable but I just couldn't stop myself.

As I have said, George used to threw clothes around and indulge in other antisocial behaviour, such as pulling knitting off needles, for which I was blamed. There was a nine-year age gap between my older sister and myself and, of course, she had a wardrobe of lovely clothes, including a beautiful cheesecloth dress. This was found with a large yellow stain on it, as if someone had thrown a curry at it and, of course, I got the blame, although I would never have damaged it, I really loved it.

My father thought talk about a ghost was gobbledegoo until one night he had to sleep in the spare room, then he opened his eyes to find himself staring up into the face of a ghostly Cavalier. The Cavalier was standing in the centre of the bed, right in the middle of my father, looking down at him. My father punched out but the blows went straight through him. The Cavalier didn't go immediately but gradually faded away.

By this time we had lived in the house for three years and my parents decided that they needed to do some investigating about George. They went to see the woman who lived there previously. She said, 'Why do you think I wanted to move?' She had heard the tapping and the footsteps, and once she had seen an apparition with a face which looked as if it were made from papier mache. She had decided to ask for a transfer when she had seen a dark, shadowy figure and her two-year old son had run straight through it.

The house was semi-detached so mother went to see the next-door neighbour on the adjoining side. She had heard nothing out of the ordinary but had seen a very curious phenomenon several times – that of a ten feet by five feet burning crucifix on the adjoining wall.

My parents went to see the Assistant Housing Manager at the Council who didn't bat an eyelid, he had heard of the house's reputation. We moved a short distance away. Mother could see our old house from her bedroom window and she would often stand there, watching our old house, convinced that George would try to find her. But he never did.

Interestingly, the woman who moved into the house when we left had a nervous breakdown.

Old fishponds, Bordesley Abbey Meadows.

REDDITCH

The black dog of Arden

 N 1312 THE WHITE-ROBED MONKS of Bordesley Abbey gave sanctuary to the earl of Warwick who sought refuge from the anger of Edward II. The earl had committed the unforgivable sin of executing Piers Gaveston, the king's favourite and foster brother. Gaveston's insolence to the powerful barons had turned them against him. He had nicknamed the earl of Warwick 'the black dog of Arden', to which the Earl had replied that Gaveston would one day feel his teeth. Feelings had been so intense that they had almost led to a civil war and Gaveston had been forced to leave England. On his return, he had been seized by the earl of Warwick and beheaded (the earl maintained accidentally) on Blacklow Hill, just outside Warwick.

Sanctuary saved the earl from the wrath of the prince but it did not protect him from Gaveston's friends who poisoned him the following year. He was buried in the prestigious Bordesley Abbey.

All that is now left of this great Cistercian abbey which played so prominent a part in the history of England, is a series of attractive meadows. These were once a marshy swamp, then about 1140 eleven monks arrived to drain the land and begin the building of Bordesley abbey. Just outside the abbey precinct, not far from a small stream tinted with red oxide, a group of stonemasons settled to help with the construction of the abbey and this was the beginning of Red-ditch.

There are many rumours of ghostly black dogs and phantom monks on the Bordesley Abbey meadows. James Woodward was one of the first to recognise the value of the site in the 1860's and he excavated some tiles and a coffin which he assumed belonged to the Black Dog of Arden. He was nervously keeping watch over these artefacts when:

> St Stephen's clock, striking the hour of midnight, intensified rather than disturbed my train of thought, when a louder blast of wind caused me to raise my head – at that instant another head appeared above the heap of soil on the opposite side of the Chapel – it was the head of a large black dog. It looked at me for a moment, and then disappeared. I seized a crow-bar and climbed to the top of the mound but my visitor was gone.

He was not the only one to see the apparition, his assistant, Twinning, had caught sight of it earlier in the evening.

The flat-footed monk

Part of the monks' fishponds still exist in the Bordesley meadows as a small stretch of water inhabited by mallards, moorhens and a variety of wildlife. This is an attractive area by day but when night begins to fall it can become lonely and eerie. Mrs Dale of Church Hill describes her experiences one winter evening.

I've lived in this area for 15 years but have not been particularly interested in Bordesley Abbey because I was working full-time and this didn't leave me time for anything else.

Anyway, one winter's evening in November 1992, I came down Easemore Road and along the back of the prefabs to where the public path crosses over the river and on past the farm. I then followed the path until I reached the two Bordesley Abbey fishponds which are crossed by a little bridge. It was dusk and I was hurrying to reach Church Hill before it became dark. There is the intermittent lamp but the pathway is, on the whole, poorly lit.

Suddenly, I noticed a very tall, thin gentleman in front of me, walking away from me and towards the ponds. Although he was about fifty yards ahead, the atmosphere was cold and sharp so that I could see him quite clearly. He was wearing a black gown which was not at all flowing or baggy but straight down, almost fitted, to me he looked like a monk. I could not see his head so I assumed that this was bent over as he hurried. The peculiar thing about him which made me think that all was not quite normal was the determined manner in which he walked, with long, flat-footed strides, straight towards the fishponds.

I felt quite nervous and frightened. I reached the end of the public path but he was nowhere in sight. I turned and looked back, wondering where he had gone. I could see for some distance across the grass and over the golf course but he was nowhere in sight.

This was the second time I had seen something peculiar at that point. When I was a little girl I sat down on this bridge on the way home from school and I heard heavy footsteps on the bridge and a shadow blocked out the sun. I turned round but nothing was there.

A curious fact is that, although the monks of Bordesley Abbey were Cistercian and wore a white habit, ghostly monks only seem to wear black or brown.

A witching time of night

Elaine Winters*

Elaine works in the offices of the Redditch Borough Council. The apparition was seen by both Elaine and her children, giving an interesting double sighting. The A441 at this point runs quite close to the Bordesley Abbey Meadows – if the dark shape had been that of a monk or a black dog there would have been some faint logic, but instead they caught sight of something totally inexplicable. Elaine gives her version first.

I'm not into the paranormal, I don't know if was a ghost that I saw, I can only tell you exactly what happened.

I was driving along the A441 at about half past eight one winter evening in 1990, going from Redditch to Alvechurch. I was driving past the Abbey Stadium, which was on my right, and I had just reached the point where the houses end on the left, when suddenly, this person in a long black cloak appeared looking just like the archetypal witch. It was just a long, black shape so I couldn't see a face but it appeared to have a female form. It looked as if it was going to step out into the road so I swerved out of her path, fortunately nothing was going the other way and there was no other traffic around. I looked in my mirror to see who it was but I couldn't see anything. I turned round and looked but nothing was there.

The kids were in the car with me and I said, 'That was weird, did you see that!'. They told me that they had seen it. We talked about it a lot afterwards.

Elaine's children are represented here by her daughter, Deborah.

After finishing drama quite late one night, my mother collected me from the Palace Theatre in Redditch. It was a clear night, due to the rain having just stopped as we turned into the Birmingham Road from the direction of Sainsbury's supermarket. We drove along, the car approaching the bend in the road, just past the bus stop on the left, when I became aware of a presence of something on the left-hand side of the road, although at first I did not take any particular notice of it.

Travelling another couple of metres along, directly opposite the Abbey Stadium's sports centre, the object on the side of the road suddenly made a move by stepping straight into the path of our car, as if had been waiting for us, causing my mother to swerve suddenly to the other side of the road.

I noticed that this 'object' was a figure wearing a black cloak which covered it from head to foot. The face was obscured entirely by the hood and no arms, hands, legs or feet were visible either, it just appeared to float across the road in front of us.

As our car swung across the road, I turned back to continue observing the figure, who did not turn back but continued straight on as if towards the Abbey Stadium playing fields. As I was still observing the figure it suddenly vanished not far from the edge of the road, and there was no sign that it had been there at all.

Grace and favour and the gamekeepers cottage

The Abbey fell into decline after the black death and by the time of Henry VIII there was very little left to dissolve. The local inhabitants grabbed any stones and timbers for house-building so that the building became little more than a ruin. Then, in 1542, Lord Windsor arrived at the ruins with his retinue to take up residence. What had happened was that Henry VIII had sent for him, and to the latter's amazement, had announced that he wanted to exchange Lord Windsor's handsome home, already stocked with provisions for Christmas, for Bordesley Abbey and its estates. It had been apparent that if Lord Windsor wanted to keep his head on his shoulders, he should comply with the king's request. He arrived with his retinue on a cold, wet, November evening to find the abbey inhabitable. Fortunately, one of the Abbey's granges was nearby, Hewell Grange, and Lord Windsor settled there.

Hewell Grange was rebuilt in 1884 and a series of outbuildings were erected. One of these was a game-keeper's cottage in Salters Lane. On the sale of the estate it became a rented cottage.

Mrs Mitchell★ has lived in Redditch all her life and is well-known locally as her work brings her into contact with the public. She married in 1963 and moved into the gamekeeper's cottage. It was a young bride's dream, a picturesque country home with all mod cons. However, the cottage was not as idyllic as it first seemed…

Part of the house, such as the bathroom, had been built on but the rest of the house was very old. Some of the rooms, such as the hallway, the stairs and our bedroom gave me an eerie feeling and our bedroom always seemed inexplicably cold. Odd things often happened in that house. I remember lying in bed and watching the bedroom door slowly and deliberately close. Once we returned to the house and found the trapdoor into the loft pulled to one side. We asked our next-door neighbour if he had moved it – he laughed and pointed out that with his arthritic hip, there was no way in which he could reach it. Another time, we heard such a heavy bump in the loft that my husband got the ladder out to see what was going on, but there was nothing there. That was the only time my husband took any notice of my suggestion that the house was haunted.

One night, I woke up and the moon was shining through the bedroom window. In the moonlight I saw an old man kneeling and praying. He was very old and very tiny, had he stood up he would not have been more than five feet three. He had a woollen cap pulled on his head, otherwise his clothes were very ordinary. I shouted for my husband to wake up and reached for the light cord which hung over the bed but by the time I was able to put on the light the old man had disappeared. My husband said that I must have been dreaming, but to me it seemed very real.

Ten years later my husband was in one of the locals when he saw a man whom he recognised as having moved into the gamekeeper's cottage after us. He went over and made himself known. The man remarked, 'We've moved from that house now, and were we glad to get out, my wife always declared it was haunted!

Unfortunately, my husband did not get his address and has not seen him since but I would love to know if his wife's experiences were the same as mine.

It is said that Lord Windsor laid the foundations for the needle industry to develop in Redditch.

Through the eye of a needle

There's an old Redditch tale that, in the early 1900's, an American needle man-ufacturer sent a very fine needle to Redditch with a note, 'Beat that!'. A Redditch manufacturer promptly made a needle which could pass through the eye of the American needle. Although this story is unlikely to be true, it does illustrate the pride of Redditch folk in their expertise in needle manufacturing. Redditch and its outlying villages are famous world-wide for their needles, springs and fish-hooks. The industry came to Redditch in Elizabethan times when needle-makers migrated here from Buckinghamshire, probably attracted by the emery stones in the river Arrow. By 1800, 400 people were employed in Redditch with 2,000 in the neighbourhood. At first this was a cottage industry, but in the late 1820's heavy water-powered machinery was introduced and workers had to move into factories.

They voiced their objections in the 1830 riots when machinery was smashed and eight men were arrested. Despite their unpopularity, the mills were highly successful and between 1841 and 1861, the population of Redditch doubled.

Forge Mill, on the Bordesley Abbey site, has been preserved as a working museum. Other mills have not been so fortunate and those which have not been demolished have been converted into quaint houses or hostelries.

Forge Mill, Redditch

At the rear of a Georgian residence on the Worcestershire/Warwickshire border is a two-storey needlemill. In this workshop needle pointers worked from the first light of the dawn until the last rays of the sun had disappeared. Their wages were more than twice the average to recompense for the fact that most of them died from pneumoconiosis before they were thirty. The present owner has an unusual story.

By 1957 the needlemill had fallen into disrepair so my father and I rebuilt it, using the same bricks and timbers, with one large room below and one above. We modified the ground floor slightly by inserting a French window to bring in more light, but the room on the first floor remains rather dark, as it contains a good many old timbers. It has one window overlooking the flood gates, beneath that window is a spare bed and when I sleep there I have, on occasion, had a most strange experience.

The first time was during the summer of 1958. I go to sleep very quickly and I sleep quite heavily, but I woke up in the middle of the night to find myself halfway out of the window and just about to step out! I had this urge to get out of the window and I thought I was on the ground floor! Fortunately, the cold air woke me up as the drop is about twelve feet – enough for quite a nasty injury! Strange to say, I had no sense of fear.

About a year later I slept in the bed again. There were two candlesticks on the window sill and when I woke up the next morning I found them under my bed. I then remembered that again, during the night, I had felt compelled to get out of the bedroom window and had moved the candlesticks to clear the decks for action. Fortunately, I must have had the good sense to return to my bed. After that I moved my bed over to the other side of the room and I had no more problems until I slept in there again. Once more in the middle of the night I felt driven to get out of the window, so much so that I started up with such force that I broke the bed! The wooden panel at the foot of the bed was smashed in two.

I have slept in that bed under the window many times and on some occasions I have felt compelled to go through the window. I cannot think of an explanation for this, I am not depressed by the dark and I am not subject to nightmares. Nothing similar has ever happened to me anywhere else. I must emphasise that I had no sense of a presence, just this compulsion to get out of the window.

William Avery's Victorian collection of ghost stories in Redditch library tells of another needlemaker's ghost which appeared in a Studley cottage one beautiful sunny Sunday morning.

My neighbour was then but young, and lay in bed after the rest of the household had gone downstairs. 'I was not asleep or dozing, but wide awake,' says he, 'when I saw my brother-in-law, a needle pointer, enter the room in his working dress of corduroy. He passed by my bedside, and vanished through the closed window of the room. I called my mother and told her what I had seen. She replied that I must have been mistaken, but my brother-in-law died the week after, nevertheless'.

Chloe and the choirboys

Until the 1800's the little chapel of St Stephens, the only part of Bordesley Abbey left standing, served the people of Redditch but in 1854 it was demolished and the materials used to build a much larger church in the centre of the town, also known as St Stephens. This was followed, twenty-two years later, by St George's, the architect being F Preedy, who built or partly rebuilt about thirty other churches in Worcestershire. St George's is a building which was never quite finished. There was evidently intended to be some carving round the tops of the pillars but it was never completed. Perhaps the craftsmen were frightened away by strange noises and a ghostly figure – the church has long had a reputation for being haunted. The ghost was christened Chloe in about 1983, when the vicar, who was working in the vicarage, heard a lady singing in another room. He hurried in to see who it was but no-one was there.

That the ghost was female was confirmed in 1990, when a church member who was walking towards St George's saw a lady in Edwardian dress standing outside the west door. Two parishioners have also encountered Chloe, Philip Jarvis and Rod Laight. Philip is a railway enthusiast but it was his second hobby, that of playing church organs, which made him aware of the ghost.

> I have been playing the organ since it was first installed in 1964. When I started practising – sometimes until ten o'clock at night, I realised I was not alone in the church. One night, I heard someone come in through the doors at the western end. There's no mistaking the noise. These are double doors, an ancient outer door and an inner, newer one. Both doors make a noise, the outer one is heavy and grinds open and the inner one creaks. I was very surprised because I had locked the outer door from the inside, so I stopped playing and went to see who was there. The church was empty and the door was still locked.

Rod Laight describes a thriving pre-1960's Church of England.

> My friends now may find it difficult to believe but I was once a choirboy at St George's Church in Redditch. In those days there was a very large choir, lots of Redditch families went, and we met twice a week for choir practice. The choirmaster was Mr Morgan and sometimes we had an informal practice where we all sat round the organ. That's when we heard tales of a ghost, mainly about the noises that people could hear when the church was empty.
>
> After choir practice, we often played table tennis in the Vicar's garage,

and so, one dark winter's night in 1958, it was about nine o'clock before we started to disperse. About half-a-dozen of us were just going out of the main gate, when one of the boys said, 'Look!' and pointed upwards. There, right high up, peering over a buttress was a white misty face without any apparent features. It had something black on its head which we assumed was a hat – it could have been a bowler hat. The wall was straight up – it was impossible for anyone to climb up there.

We ran along St George's road to the telephone box and telephoned the Rev Walters. He had quite a fierce dog and he let it out, but it wouldn't go anywhere near the part of the church where we had seen the head. We assumed it had seen some kind of apparition.

The haunted shopping centre

In 1964, to the consternation of its residents, Redditch was designated as a new town. The Redditch Development Corporation was formed to expand the population from 29,000 to 90,000 with the Birmingham overspill in mind. The Corporation was appalled to discover that blueprints for new towns were virtually non-existent and almost everything needed to be worked out from scratch. Consequently, Redditch has the first computer-designed roads and the clover-leaf junction which joins the Alcester, Alvechurch, Warwick and Bromsgrove Highways was the first in the United Kingdom.

The Rt Hon Richard Crossman became Minister of Housing and Local Government in 1964 and in his diaries is an entry, 'A fairly free day except that I hd to spend two hours listening to the Redditch Labour Party telling me what a bloody awful New Town the Ministry had wished upon them'. Nevertheless, the Redditch Development Corporation managed to produce an attractive and comfortable new town.

The shopping centre at Redditch was very nearly not built as we know it. The Chief Architect had a nervous breakdown when the centre had been partially completed and was away for six months, leaving the project in the hands of the Finance Manager. When he returned, he found that the designs had undergone a radical cost-cutting exercise with the result that it was very different to the original specifications. He arrived back at work just in time to rescue it.

With the new shopping centre came Worcestershire's most popular ghosts[†]. An inspector for Phillip's Security who worked on the site from 1981 to 1985, commented, 'I have worked at many, many different sites across the country and I have never come across anything, anywhere, in any way similar to the incidents at the Kingfisher Centre'. He describes two incidents as follows:

A cleaning technician was operating a large cleaning machine one evening at the bottom of the first escalator leading to the bus station. He was working behind the glass door to the car park opposite the bus station, when he saw a dark shadow on the far side of the glass. He pulled the machine to one side and, thinking the shape was that of a police officer or security guard, beckoned it through. The dark shadow came through the door, through the machine and through him. He left the machine and ran yelling and shouting to the staff in the Centre.

In a second incident, a security guard was patrolling the balcony outside Owen Owen's store at midnight when he saw the dark shape of 'a guy in a robe-shaped thing' gliding rapidly towards him. He rushed to the lift, tumbled inside and breathed a sigh of relief as the lift started to go down but then he saw, in the mirrors, that the ghost was in the lift with him. Fortunately the apparition remained stationery so that the lift went through it and left it behind. The guard refused to patrol the balcony after that and as Phillip's Security said that they could not employ someone who would only do half a round, they parted company.

By popular demand, here are yet two more tales from the early days of the haunted centre.

Pottery plus poltergeist

Stella★ worked at Pottery Plus for four to five months during the summer of 1991. She was friendly with another girl, Victoria★, and the paranormal events occurred to both of them.

I had heard rumours that the place was haunted before I started working there. Someone told me that one afternoon, a heavy shelf had flown across the room. While I was there some weird things happened, always downstairs in the basement. Occasionally, we would go in and find leaflets arranged in a fan on the floor. Once, Victoria was stacking plates and when she turned round, the plates which she had left on the floor had arranged themselves in a circle round her feet.

The worst thing was the footsteps. They were quite light, perhaps a ladies' footsteps, and could be heard walking up and down the stairs often as much as four times a day, usually in the afternoon.

On one occasion when the shop upstairs was full of customers, we heard a shout from the basement. It sounded like a woman's cry and went on for about a minute. All the customers said, 'What's that?'. The manager thought it was a customer who had strayed downstairs and sent me down to investigate but there was no-one in the basement at all.

Another weird thing happened one morning when I was away but Victoria told me about it afterwards. There was one cupboard which was kept locked as it held the precious Royal Doulton. The staff arrived at work to find that a Royal Doulton figure had been removed from the cabinet and was standing on the shelf next to the plates. The cupboard was checked but it was still locked.

Sales assistant tells all

Daphne Weaver*

I started work at one of the larger stores when it opened in 1981 and I can tell you several incidents about their ghost.

In a certain area of the store several of the staff have heard someone calling their name, but when they look around to see who is calling, no-one is about. Occasionally, a customer remarks that they have a strange feeling in this part of the store and one of our managers, who sometimes has to work alone in the store after the shop is closed, says that he feels uneasy about working there.

I think it was in 1988 that a friend of mine, who is very sensible and level-headed, saw a brown shape, most of it looking quite solid, standing in this same area. It was as large as a man, it seemed to hover just above the ground and its head seemed to be draped in a hood or a cowl. It was only a couple of feet away and she could see the texture of the fabric quite clearly. It was a rough fabric, like a coarse hessian.

Strange to say, she did not seem to be at all frightened by this experience but seemed to become quite attached to the ghost and protective of it. She told me to keep quiet and not to tell anyone about it, although she doesn't mind its existence being put on record.

Another member of staff (who has since left) did not believe in ghosts and thought the incident quite silly, but about two years later she had a similar experience. She was bending down when she felt someone bending over her. Looking round, she caught sight of a brown shape with the same coarse texture of material. This member of staff was very frightened.

Only last week I, myself, heard my name being called. I can't say whether the voice was male or female, it was not that distinct. Afterwards I wondered if I had imagined it but at the time I was so sure it was my name that I turned round to see who was calling. Last week was the beginning of Lent and other members of staff tell me that the voice is at its most active in Lent and at Easter.

Shoppers at the Redditch Centre will be pleased to hear that the paranormal incidents have now died down and very little has been reported during the past few years.

The invisible bookworm

When the new library in Redditch was opened in 1976, it came as something of a surprise to the Redditch folk, because it was so very different to the old. It had previously been situated in a dark and poky Victorian building on the corner of Church Road and Church Green West and the purpose-designed premises to which it moved were light and spacious. However, it has not been the old Victorian building which provided a ghost but the new premises. The librarians, after reading and lending tales of other people's ghosts with interest and some amusement, were rather taken aback when they found that they had one of their own.

In 1992, the caretaker of the Food Hall, which was then next door to the library, was sweeping up at the end of a day's business when he noticed a dark shadow pass across a library window. The next morning, he mentioned this to one of the librarians. At first the staff suspected a burglary but there was no sign of any break-in. The incident was forgotten, but about eighteen months later a series of bizarre incidents brought it to mind.

A senior librarian was not very pleased to hear the lifts whizzing up and down during his evening poetry readings. Evans Lifts were called in several times but could find nothing wrong. Furthermore, they said it was impossible for the lift to start up on its own.

Shortly afterwards a library assistant reported:

The bindery is a small room off the main basement, fitted with metal books stacks which reach from floor to ceiling. On Friday, 24 February 1994 at about 2 pm, I was working alone there, checking books returned from the binders, and everything was very quiet. As I stood there, with my back to the bookcases, someone breathed heavily over my left shoulder. I heard the breath exhale and felt it across my neck. Thinking that someone had crept up on me and was playing a joke I turned quickly, but no-one was there. Then a second heavy breath emitted from somewhere between the stacks. When a third, snatched breath, like a stifled sob, the sort you might sometimes let out

I could not have shouted out. I was rigid. It was very real and I can find no explanation for it.

A few days later the Administration Assistant needed to move a word processor but as she picked it up and held it tightly in her arms, it started to vibrate. She thought she must have left it plugged in but a quick glance showed that the plug was hanging free. This was not her only unusual experience.

Sometimes I am last out of the building and I leave through the back door of the basement. I usually have quite a heavy shopping bag and would like to use the lift to the basement but it's dangerous for me to do so when I am in the building on my own, in case the lift develops some fault such as failing to open or jamming between floors.

Consequently, to avoid carrying my shopping bag down the stairs, I put my bag in the lift then send it down to the basement, walking down the stairs to meet it and turning off the lights as I go. The lift usually arrives just before I do, then I open the doors, collect my bag and exit through the back door of the building just as the lift doors are starting to close. Several times recently, just as I have been going out of the back door I have looked back and seen a dark shadow either coming in or going out of the lift. This sends cold shivers down my back! It's nothing precise, just a greyish impression like a dark cloud, and is the same every time.

Most of these events occurred over a period of a few months, then faded away as mysteriously as they had arrived.

Taken for a ride

The next story from the centre of Redditch is written by Don Draycott. Here is no black dog, monk or witch, just an entity who loves a trip on a bus.

Many Redditch folk will remember Mr Cyril Atkins and 'Renown Coaches' at the bottom of Melen Street. I worked for Cyril from 1960 to 1963. During this time many vehicles came and went but one which I will never forget was JOM 166, a Leyland half cab. It arrived at Melen Street one morning in a sorry condition. Mr Atkins said, 'We'll do it up for works' and school trips'. When new, it had belonged to Smiths Coaches, Birmingham, but had since had many owners including a builder and an engineering works. After four or five weeks, it was painted, polished and overhauled and gleamed like a fire engine. 'That's mine' said Bill Wooton. No-one else wanted it so it was 'Bill's bus'!

Summer passed and with darker days it was noted that Bill drove with all the interior lights on even when empty. Some remarked, 'Bill's afraid of the dark'. One dark morning at ten to six I arrived at the garage and rolled back the doors to find my bus in the back row. Bill's bus was in the door. 'I'll take Bill's bus!' I thought. I climbed into the cab, thumbed the starter and we were off – empty with no interior lights.

I was just passing Alvechurch Football Club when someone tapped on the glass behind me. I thought, 'Bill's left a drunk on board from last night!'. I stopped, switched on the light, went round to the coachside door and looked in – no-one. I searched the bus – empty. Back in the cab I switched all the lights off and continued to Birmingham. Coming up Hopwood Hill there was a frantic knocking on the bulkhead glass. I stopped, put the lights on and again searched the bus. Nothing! This time the lights stayed on and there was no further trouble. I told no-one what had happened.

One Saturday night the following summer, we all arrived back at Melen Street at the same time. 'Let's go for a drink' was suggested. There were six of us drinking in the Windsor Club in Windsor Street. Someone fetched another round and Andy said, all serious, 'I will tell you a story and if you laugh or call me a liar you will be for it!'

As Andy began his tale I went cold. His story was exactly like my experience with the old bus. When the story was finished there was silence for a moment. Then, 'That happened to me', 'And me' said another. Every man at that table had experienced the same thing with the old bus.

Where is it now? Gone for scrap? Or is it haunting some bus museum?

The haunted football club

At the Redditch end of Bromsgrove Road, next to the Hillview Medical Centre, is a modest drive with the discreet sign of Redditch Football Club. Many people don't realise that this drive opens out into the large sporting complex. The club moved there in 1951 although the present buildings date from 1969. The football pitch is edged with waist-height hoarding pasted with colourful advertisements, and running along one side of the pitch is a long, two-storey building. A viewing gallery runs the length of the building, behind it are a network of offices, meeting rooms and a large function room with a bar. Halfway along this building is a tunnel, sloping gently downwards, leading from the pitch to the changing rooms. The Redditch Football Club have three teams, Senior, Reserve and Youth, and they also take other local teams under their umbrella, such as the Kingfisher Colts. The work of Redditch Football Club is held in high regard by the profession and guests have included George Best, Billy Bremner, Jack Charlton and Dennis Law with Ray Clements currently on the invitation list.

Dennis Rawlings, the Social Club Manager, says that something strange has been going on at the club for the past few years.

It's ever since Sid passed away. We have a lot of elderly football enthusiasts who come in to help and Sid was among the best. He spent a lot of time here, he was a wise and knowledgeable bloke with a great sense of humour. Most of his work was done in the little room which we use as a kitchen and it's in that area that these weird things occur. Next door is a room known as the cellar, we keep the gas cylinders for the bar in here and we keep finding them turned off. It's quite difficult to do this and you couldn't turn them off by accident. The room next to that is the ladies' toilets and there the hand dryer turns itself on for absolutely no reason and no-one can find anything wrong with it. However, we also have curious incidents taking place right through the building. Our Secretary was clearing the dressing room with his son when the son felt a tap on his shoulder, thinking it was his father, he turned round and was amazed to see that no-one was there. When these things happen we say, 'Sid's around!'

The main incident happened on Friday, 19th May 1995, when the weather was quite warm. We hire our rooms out for private functions and on the night in question, the Kingfisher Colts (the eleven-year olds) were using the function room for their end-of-season presentation. It's a grand event with about 200 people there, parents are invited and they have a meal and a discotheque. The kids had got fed up with the disco and were running around the premises. Although it was late in the evening and dark, a dozen or so were playing on the football pitch. I expect the fresh air made a welcome change from the noise and cigarette smoke indoors. I was working behind the bar when I became aware of a commotion, so much so that I heard it above the noise of the disco. Evidently, the boys had come running in, saying that a white shape had come across the pitch toward them and gone into the tunnel to the dressing rooms. The lads were quite frightened, whatever they saw was beyond a boy's imagination, and one of them refused to go back outside again.

This is not the first time a white shape has been seen on the pitch. A year or two before we were having a Country and Western and the kids then said that they had seen something on the pitch, although they didn't show the same fear as the lads in this last incident.

Rod Laight has been Director and Chief Executive of Redditch Football Club for the past three years.

We have two Junior teams, the Kingfisher Colts and Crabbs Cross boys, aged 8 – 15. In May we have two presentation evenings, the one about three weeks after the other. The boys are running round the club quite freely, inside and outside, until it's quite dark. Suddenly, a number of them came hurtling in and I spoke to the parents to see what was the matter. They said that they were in the main stand when a white misty shape came from the other side of the field across the pitch towards them, disappearing down the players' tunnel. The boys were ashen faced and very scared.

About three weeks later Dennis Rawlings said exactly the same thing had happened again at the second presentation. A white apparition had appeared on the far side of the pitch and again frightened the boys.

I have asked around some of the older members and their reaction is that they are not surprised that the pitch is haunted. Several of the oldest members who have now passed away had a dear love of the football club and would spend all their time either on pitch work or improving the changing rooms. They're not surprised that one of them is reluctant to leave the place that he was so fond of!

The next narrative has been compiled from an interview with Daniel, Mark, Lee, James, Anthony and Scott of the Kingfisher Colts.

About seven of us were playing football on the pitch and although it was dark, the field was floodlit. You can only get into the field from the gate behind us and we were playing there for quite a long time so that we knew we were the only ones there. Suddenly there was a massive flash as if a fire-work was being let off and there was a lot of little sparks in two places, one lot in the stands and another on this particular place on the pitch. Then Daniel shouted, 'Hey, look, something's over there' and we saw the shape of a man moving across the football pitch. We couldn't see it all that well but he seemed to have a round head and a cloak that went down to the ground. One very peculiar thing was that he had very large feet. The lights were on at the other side of the pitch so that they were shining on to the back of it so that the edge of it was lit up but you could see the lights shining through it as well. First of all we thought it was someone playing a joke but when we realised that it wasn't a person we ran on to the pitch and started throwing stones at it. The stones seemed to go right through it so we legged it back indoors. The ghost went into the players' tunnel.

There were strange noises as well, the windows in the stands were banging as if someone was hammering them and we could hear footsteps running round the dressing rooms, although they were locked up and we knew nobody was in there. It sounded like a little kid running round in football boots.

We told our parents that we had seen a ghost but they just laughed and told us to stop fooling around. When the others heard that a ghost was outside, they rushed out to see it so we went with them. This time, the shape was in the stands. Some of our parents came out to see what was going on but by that time, the ghost had gone.

Two of the boys saw more than a shape. This is to be expected, when an entity appears to a group, some only see a shadow while others see the ghost in detail.

We saw this man on the pitch, we could see his face, he had grey hair and his face was wrinkled. When we went out for a second time, the man was there again but this time he was in the stands. He slowly faded away, he probably took about twelve seconds to fade.

Three weeks later a second presentation evening was held for thirteen-year olds. Many of these older footballers have now left the club, but two said that they had caught a glimpse of a shadow standing on the pitch. The majority of those present made some remark about the strange noises coming from the locked dressing rooms. One lad said, 'It sounded as if doors were banging and as if there was a whole army tramping around there in football boots!'

CRABBS CROSS

RABBS CROSS IS ONE OF THE OLD SUBURBS of Redditch, as local motorists are only too aware. The roads to Stratford, Evesham, Bromsgrove, Redditch and Birmingham all converge on Crabbs Cross island without the benefit of a New Town traffic system to assist the flow, resulting in long queues during the rush hour.

Some of the older residents still speak of the island as 'Boney's island'. James Woodward, a local tutor, wrote in 1886:

> After asking many persons why the above term applied to Crabbs Cross, I have found the general opinion to be that it was on account of this spot being a favourite locality for fights some forty or fifty years ago. Being situated on the border of two counties, a change of ground from one county to another placed the combatants out of the jurisdiction of the local magistrates.

That is, if a fight was stopped on one side of the island, the combatants had only to step a few yards over to the other side, which was in another county, to be able to continue.

The greatest villain in Redditch lived at Crabbs Cross – Old Crowther. He was known to be the perpetrator of every shady deal although he specialised in stolen needles. It was even said that the devil used to visit him in a local hollow known as Fish Ponds. He lived in Littlewoods but he owned a row of houses on the main Evesham Road which he let to his conspirators. They were not divided in the attic so that if one house contained stolen goods, and the premises were raided, the goods could be hastily transferred to a house the other end.

His wife held him in great affection and died before him, caring for him even after her death as the following story shows, published under Notes and Queries in the Redditch Advertiser on 27 December 1886.

> Old Crowther… had planned a robbery somewhere beyond Hunt End and he and another were on their way down Littlewoods to effect it when the figure of a woman appeared before them with upraised hand. It came nearer and they could just see in the dimness the palled features of the dead Mrs Crowther. The ghost addressed her (husband), telling him for his own sake to return, for their intended robbery was known.

Local residents are now extremely respectable and as Crabbs Cross is next to the green belt, the building land in the area sells for some of the highest prices in Redditch. Among the inhabitants is Joan Patterson, a school dinner lady, well known locally for her charitable work, and with a tale to tell about the Crabbs Cross apparition.

> When I was a little girl I was playing with a group of friends halfway down the hill below Crabbs Cross Methodist Church. It was an old building then and it has since been rebuilt. We were halfway between the shops and the church when suddenly, a white shape appeared from the church and floated gently across the road, disappearing into the hedge on the other side. It was just a solid white irregular shape, about two-and-a-half feet deep and three or four feet wide. We all shouted, 'a ghost!', 'a ghost!' and ran off. I told my grandfather later and he said that it must have been a piece of paper blowing about. It was much too large to be a newspaper, or even an owl.

LAKESIDE

The river Arrow meanders pleasantly from its source in the Lickey Hills through the valley of Redditch to Alcester. Before the development of the new town the building of industries along the river between Studley and Redditch caused the river to flood occasionally. To prevent this, the Arrow Valley Lake was created in the early 1970's. As Gordon Anstis remarked, 'This was to prove an inspirational feature in a lovely natural park which effectively bonded the old and new parts of Redditch'.

Lakeside lies to the west of the lake and is a later development of the new town. It was here that Jim Knight's★ friend had an attractive semi-detached house.

A friend of mine lived in a haunted house at Lakeside. When I went to visit him at the end of 1984, his daughter, Samantha, came to the door and asked me to check out the loft bedroom. She said that something had grabbed her by the hair and pulled her off the bed. The main part of the loft had been converted into a third storey bedroom, with a staircase going up to it and two doors side by side, the one going into the old part of the loft which contained the hot water tank, the other into her bedroom.

This had been the culmination of a series of strange incidents. A can had flown across the room to hit someone on the head. My friend had been in the house on his own when he had heard thumping coming down the stairs. He thought it was the cat but a rubber ball had suddenly taken upon itself to start rolling down the stairs and thump hard on each stair. Three of us had been sitting on the settee when an invisible someone had given my friend a shove from behind.

All the activity seemed to emanate from this new room in the loft so he nailed the door to the frame by hammering in a series of heavy nails at an angle. The next time I saw him, he was as white as a sheet. All the nails had been pushed out from the inside and were lying on the floor.

He wondered if someone could have entered the loft in some way, he therefore drilled a spy hole in the centre of the door in order to look inside. So that no-one could look out, he wedged a pen in the hole. While he watched he saw the pen twist and spiral its way out and drop to the floor. He again inserted the pen and again it twisted and dropped out.

I was standing outside the house one evening when I knew that it was empty and I happened to look up to see a transparent silhouette of a man looking out of the loft window. He seemed to be of average height and build but the strange thing was that he seemed to be a World War II figure, the sort you see in picture books, with an air warden's hat on and wearing a gas mask. Another evening, someone else in the house was going towards the bathroom when he saw a white figure standing by the bathroom door. It was like a negative picture, white on black, and it was just distinct enough for him to make out female features.

My friend had the house exorcised three times without effect then suddenly, for no apparent reason, the manifestations stopped as suddenly as they had begun.

PARK FARM SOUTH

Maurice Wells' thought-provoking narrative takes place on the borders of Warwickshire and Worcestershire, near the Leys High School and the Alexandra Hospital.

I was born in Studley and although I moved to Redditch when I was small, much of my social life and many of my friends were at Studley. Towards the end of the summer in 1968, when I was eighteen, I was driving home after playing basketball at Studley Youth Club, when something happened which scared the life out of me.

It was quite dark, sometime between 10 and 10.30 in the evening. As I drove round the double bend (which has now been straightened out slightly) on the Warwickshire/Worcestershire border by the Griffin Inn, my headlights picked out a man with his back towards me, walking on the left-hand side of the road towards Redditch. I could see him quite clearly and I noticed that he was dressed in very distinctive clothing – he was wearing a tweedy, sporty-type jacket and trousers with a large check pattern. He was a very short man, not more than five feet tall, quite stocky and elderly.

As I drove up close to him with the headlights shining brightly on his check trousers, he suddenly disappeared. I was a bit shocked but didn't take it too seriously. I thought it could be a trick of the light or something. Then, about two or three hundred yards ahead, the same thing happened again. There, again, was the man in the check trousers. Again he disappeared as I drew near.

I must have gone pale because when I got in the house, my mother looked at me and said, 'What's the matter, you look like you've seen a ghost!' I replied, 'As a matter of fact, I think I have!'. She was very intrigued and it occurred to her that I had described a local character who had died in a house fire very near to that spot.

At the time I didn't give much thought to the experience but towards the end of 1995 it occurred to me that this had been a most unusual and interesting incident and that I should follow it up. I therefore started asking questions in the village. A number of people confirmed that a Mr Rushton, who answered my description, had once lived in a house known as 'Brooklands' almost opposite the Griffin. It was suggested that I should contact Victor Mucklow who used to work for him, and the this is Victor's report:

"Albert Rushton was an eccentric sort of man. I worked for the farmer who lived opposite at Tanhouse farm who told me that Mr Rushton had been

jilted when he was young and after that he became a recluse and would-
n't let a woman into his house. He devoted his life to horses and poultry.
He wouldn't let his fowl run on rough ground and they had their grass
cut to a certain length. He had a large shed with an oak floor and a gramo-
phone and he used to take his horses round the floor, it's said that he trained
them to dance in time to the music.

Mr Rushton was just over five feet tall and well-built. His clothes were
expensive but they were very old, and he always wore a jacket and trousers
in a very loud tweed. Most afternoons, he walked to the post box on the
Griffin wall to catch the 4 pm post. He was a pleasant enough chap and was
quite a benefactor, he gave the Redditch Council two beautiful shire horses
for their refuse collection provided they were looked after properly.

Mr Rushton used to let the farmer's sheep go on his fields at certain
times and in return, the farmer's employees had to do certain jobs for him.
I was sent across to do things like picking the thistles and stinging nettles
out of the straw for his animals, then he liked the straw bound up into
sheaves. Before you started work you were vetted by him, he wouldn't let
anybody work for him, and when you had finished he inspected your work.

I worked for him on and off for two years before he died. He told the
farmer at Tanhouse Farm that he had arthritis very badly and he was finding
that he couldn't stand the pain. He said that he kept a revolver and that if
the pain became any worse he would shoot himself. About eight o'clock in
the spring of 1955 I noticed smoke coming from the house. Someone had
already called the fire brigade, I was one of the first over there, but the house
was ablaze. One room had been full of newspapers stacked up from floor
to ceiling, so the fire had really taken hold. Mr Rushton's body was found,
fully clothed, on the first floor. The house was absolutely gutted and it was
pulled down some years afterwards".

My interest aroused, I managed to find the relevant newspaper reports
which covered almost the whole of the front page. It is interesting that the
Coroner did not conclude that Mr Rushton had shot himself despite the
fact that a cartridge was found near to where his body had been discovered
and a revolver was on the floor nearby. From my investigations it is clear
that local people believed that he had shot himself either before the fire
took hold or actually because he was trapped in the fire. Perhaps the bullet
had not killed him instantly and the smoke and carbon monoxide finished
him off. I think that this uncertainty adds to the interest of the story.

WINYATES

Winyates was built in the early 1970's when house prices had reached a scandalous £8,000. HRH Prince Richard, Duke of Gloucester, made an informal visit to Redditch and toured the Winyates area. He had VIP treatment from everyone except a certain guard dog, who, according to Gordon Anstis, 'showed no respect for high personages by biting the Royal visitor in a tender spot'. The Duke was rushed to the old Smallwood hospital, thereby receiving an opportunity to experience first hand the need for a new hospital in Redditch.

Many small children, like Stacey Lea Miles' young acquaintance, are frightened to go to bed at night. This is usually attributed to nightmares but could the phantoms sometimes be real?

A ghost has appeared to my boyfriend's brother's child since the age of three.

When this child has to go to bed he screams the place down. He says that this man stands in the corner of the room tapping his feet and holding his arms in the air, scaring him.

One evening, a neighbour was visiting the mother and as the neighbour was there for quite a time she decided to go to the loo. The toilet was opposite the bedroom and as she came out she heard the little boy crying. Seeing that she was nearest to him she did what any other person would have done and tried to open the door fully to reassure him. As she tried to open the door she felt that someone was pushing the door back so she couldn't get into the bedroom. The more she pushed the harder the door was pushed back.

The boy got out of bed and tried to get out of the room but he was being pulled away from the door. It finally took both the mother and the neighbour to get the door open.

The experience was so frightening that they are now considering moving.

WINYATES BARN

Before the new town was developed in the 1970's, the area which is now Winyates was part of the Ipsley marshes where 'bob-a-lanterns' or 'will-o-the-wisps' could be seen flitting about on a warm, humid night. The name comes from Winyates farm, consisting of an old timber barn and outbuildings. The cowsheds and outbuildings have been converted into a series of small units suitable for use by individual craftsmen, winning a *Birmingham Post* award in 1979, and the barn has become a community centre. Many local people are convinced Winyates Barn is haunted, and this is confirmed by Tom Smith, who was manager of the centre in 1992.

> I first saw our friendly visitor late in 1988, soon after the Barn opened. I passed this young gentleman on the stairs and said, 'Good morning!' I thought at the time he was rather strangely dressed. He was wearing corduroy trousers, a tan or brownish waistcoat and a collarless shirt – labourer's type clothing, I would say. He was about as tall as I am – five feet nine inches, and perhaps he was a little stocky but it was difficult to tell from the clothes he was wearing. His hair was light brown and cut into long sideburns, this was quite a distinctive feature. I realised later that there was no way in which he could have got into the building. All the doors had been locked from the inside and I was the only person in the Barn.
>
> I saw him again in January 1992. Early one morning, as soon as I arrived, I went upstairs onto the balcony and there he was, standing in the corner with his hand on my massive great Yucca plant. He was there for about five or ten seconds before he realised that I had spotted him, then he faded away.
>
> During the four years I have been Centre Manager about six or seven people have mentioned to me that they have seen the ghost. I wish now that I had kept a note of their names†.

WOODROW

The first housing project undertaken by the Redditch Development Corporation was Greenlands, followed by Woodrow, where the 1000th house was opened in 1970. Rents were between £4 and £5 per week and priority was given to key workers. This is where Stacey Lea Miles lived in 1978 when she was five years old.

> ‡I lived with my family in Pedmore Close. Strange things began to happen because my parents decided to do the Ouija board one night while we were asleep. Items went missing and pebbles were thrown at our door but no-one was there.
>
> My bed was placed so that I could see the street light shining through

---

†This was featured in Redditch Oberver of 30 December 1992.

‡Stacey Lea's story first appeared in the 1994 Hallowe'en edition of the Redditch Advertiser, as one of the best replies to a request for spooky stories.

our glass panel door on top of the landing so that it would make me sleep. One night, as I lay awake, I looked out on to the landing and saw a figure moving swiftly. I screamed so loudly my parents came running to find out what was wrong, I explained but they didn't believe me.

A few nights later I woke up screaming because someone or something had slapped me across the face. My parents came in to see why I was so upset and saw the hand print across my face. My mum didn't know what to do.

For the next month, things were quiet and nothing happened until one night, when I was trying to get to sleep, I had the feeling of being watched. I can remember being woken, I opened my eyes and at my bedside stood a black figure. All I could see was its body from the waist up, just standing there, watching me.

I froze and did not even blink. I could hear myself screaming and in came my parents. They switched the bedroom light on and I watched the figure just disappear into thin air.

I told my parents what I had seen and my mum got in touch with a local priest to bless the house. After the blessing I never experienced other hauntings.

My mum said later that my dad was joking and messing about while doing the Ouija board. I guess that upset things – but why did I get the slaps and spooks?

Harvington Hall (see page 118)

WORCESTERSHIRE FARMS AND VILLAGES

HE LANDSCAPE OF WORCESTERSHIRE is principally that of green fields bordered by hedgerows, studded with sheep and cows, and patterned with a variety of crops. The Vale of Evesham is famous world-wide for its fruit and vegetables.

However, in medieval times most of Worcestershire was covered in vast forests, stretching as far as the eye could see. Treacherous bogs and marshes could trap the unwary traveller. Wild boars roamed the forests and packs of wolves were such a nuisance that rent could be paid in wolves' heads. Any cultivated land was usually held by a community and we can still occasionally see sections of the fields that they divided into strips, each strip separated by a furrow. Gradually, the monarchy lost its hold over the forests and farming methods improved, resulting in more and more of Worcestershire being drained and cleared.

The enclosure movement transformed much of the countryside into the appearance it has today. It began in the 1400's, reaching a peak between the 1700's and 1800's. Landowners took over the open fields, turning out the families who had farmed them for centuries and divided the land into smaller fields, enclosed by hedges or walls.

ANONYMOUS LOCATION

A typical Worcestershire country village has a church dating back to Norman times, an ancient pub or two and a sprinkling of Elizabethan houses, such as Richard Carr's residence in the next story. In a country lane between Worcester and Redditch lies an attractive half-timbered house, the home of Richard Carr★. As he tells his story the dogs at his feet stretch themselves in the warmth of the coal fire and the gold of the antiques flickers in the firelight. He wears a woollen cardigan and cords which he describes as a welcome change from the pin-striped suit he has to wear during the day. He leans back, sinking into the cushions of his leather sofa.

I suppose you would say that I'm slightly psychic, or whatever word you care to use. Sometimes when the phone rings at work I know who it's going to be on the other end before I pick up the telephone. I'm not talking about people who ring up every day, but someone who goes for three or six months before ringing up.

The period concerned is from 1986 to 1988, yes, it first started mid 1986. It just happened one evening. I had retired to bed but I was restless and couldn't settle. I came down to get myself a cool orange drink. When

I came down into the lounge and walked through the area to the right of the fireplace I had a distinct feeling of cold. I knew it wasn't the cold from a draught or anything like that. It was almost as if I had walked through an icy barrier, almost like going into one of those big meat fridges. I continued into the kitchen, made myself a drink, took a sip and walked back.

When I walked through the door from the dining room into the lounge I stepped into the cold air again. I felt very apprehensive and the hairs on the back of my neck were standing erect. I closed my eyes and could see and feel in front of me a small man in his forties wearing what appeared to be blue overalls and he was pointing down at his legs. How long this took I don't know. I decided to open my eyes and continue on upstairs. As I turned to go upstairs I heard distinctly an older woman's voice calling, 'Come back! Come back!'

It was obvious that I carried the effects of this experience because my wife asked me, 'What's the matter?' I said to her, 'I have just had a most peculiar experience, I have seen a little guy in blue who was pointing down at his legs', and, 'Did you hear that woman's voice?' She said that she had not.

At that time my wife was working away from home and only here at weekends. During the following week I had a distinct impression there was somebody else in the room with me. On several occasions my left hand side became extremely cold. I assumed that this was the guy I had seen in my mind's eye. I asked him to go away and he did.

The next experience occurred one evening a week or two later when I was watching snooker on the television. I became aware of someone who appeared to be sitting stretched out parallel to me and his feet were touching mine. I immediately became very, very cold. He appeared to be sitting in a chair with his feet towards the fire like mine, watching the television. On this occasion I decided not to ask him to go away and I found if I kept my feet away from the area where he was sitting I did not feel him as much. After a while I forgot he was there.

Suddenly, out of the blue came the sound of a gentle snoring. At first I thought I was hearing things and I got out of my chair and checked to see if there were any noises coming from outside. Every so often I got the distinct noise of someone gently snoring – the sort of noise people give out when they are sitting upright in a chair. This went on for half an hour at which point I asked him again to go away and, as before, he appeared to comply with my request. The snoring stopped and the area of coldness disappeared.

By now my curiosity was aroused. I became interested in finding out who he was and why his presence was here. I knew instinctively that he was here for a purpose and that he wanted me to do something. I started to make enquiries without giving anything away as to the reason why my enquiries were made. I was most meticulous about this as I didn't want people to start making suggestions. No-one knew except my wife.

The obvious person to approach was a local lady who used to do some cleaning for me. She had lived in the area for many, many years and had actually been friends with the people who had previously lived at the cottage. When she was next here I made some excuse about wishing to know what the cottage was like in the past, where the doors were, and so on. I asked her what the position of the furniture used to be as I had heard that these entities sometimes stand in front of something that they frequently used, such as mirrors. As the area to the right of the fireplace was consistently cold and was the spot at which I had first experienced him, I thought that this might be so in this case.

There was no mirror and the furniture that was regularly used was arranged much as it is now, which would not explain the cold area. I thought I had drawn a blank. Then, quite out of the blue, she pointed to the right of the fireplace and said, 'He had his bed there when he lost his legs!'. It then transpired that the previous tenant had had his legs amputated when he was in his seventies and because he could not get up the stairs easily, his bed had been put in that very spot where there was a coldness when he was about. As I saw him when he was in his forties, he still had his legs. The reason why he pointed to them was now obvious. I also discovered that his mother used to live in a cottage just across the field. I assumed that it was her voice who was calling him back the first night that he came. I have never heard that voice again.

I continued to feel his presence and at times it was disconcerting because of the intense cold that he brought into the room when he paid us a visit. The first occasion my wife felt his presence was on the Christmas of 1986 when he appeared to join us for our Christmas dinner. In May 1987 my wife left work and remained in the cottage all the time. Although I had told her about the presence he had never visited me when she was here but always when I was on my own. Thereafter, regularly, she was aware of him. He would occasionally move away from me to my wife and she could feel his coldness just on the one side.

After this we tended to ask him to go away whenever he came. We were now into the spring of 1988. But I still had this nagging feeling that he wanted me to do something so I made enquiries and found that his widow was still living in a local village. As I looked for her name in the local telephone directory, I became aware of his presence standing next to me and

I also had a distinct feeling that he became agitated. There were two people with the same name and he seemed to tell me the right one to ring. It was most peculiar.

I started by asking the lady if she had lived with her husband at the cottage and was answered in the positive. I then told her that I had experienced the presence of her husband. Her reaction was, 'My husband is dead and he is cold in his grave. I do not wish to talk about this!'. I said to her, 'Please listen to me just for one moment, wasn't your husband's favourite colour blue, did not his mother call him from her cottage across the field, and did he not love watching sport on the television from the chair in front of the fire, but while he was watching he would often go to sleep. He wants me to tell you he's here, he's fine, he's got his legs back, he has made himself known to me, I have seen him!' At first she had sounded as if she would put the phone down but now her whole voice changed and she said, 'I wish I could believe what you are telling me'. I replied that I would not know these personal things if he had not given me the knowledge. We talked for a little while and she thanked me for ringing her. I could feel that he was standing right by the side of me during the phone call, as clear as anything. I knew then that that was what he had wanted me to do. His wife had been convinced that he was lying cold in his grave and in fact he wasn't. He had found that he could communicate with somebody (me) and he had used that ability. There is no doubt about that in my mind and I am a non-believer. I felt good, the sort of good feeling you get when you have done a good deed.

He only came back once more about two years after. I felt him quite clearly and I just said to him, 'I have done what you wanted me to do, now please go away'. His widow has now joined him and I am sure she now knows for sure.

Mrs Carr added that the first time she felt the presence, it was like walking through a cold curtain.

ALFRICK

The northern tip of the Malvern hills does not end abruptly but continues in a series of gentle wooded undulations. Here, on the edge of the Suckley Hills, is Alfrick. Very few, if any, of the present inhabitants have come face to face with a spectre but during the last century it was known as the most haunted village in Worcestershire. Fortunately, Jabez Allies, the Victorian antiquarian, was born in nearby Lulsey and was therefore on hand to record many of the strange apparitions.

His *Antiquities and Folk-lore of Worcestershire* was published in 1856, of which the following is an excerpt:

> Patch Hill, in Alfrick, lies in Patches Farm; and there is a very steep, deep and gloomy lane, called the Sandy Lane, which runs down the south side of the farm by Patch Hill to the main road... and many are the tales told of the haunted lane. Frequently has the benighted peasant been scared by the sight of a black greyhound, or of a horse or man of the same sombre hue. Sometimes a mysterious wagon, drawn by four black horses, has passed by him, while at others his eyes have encountered the form of a crow, perched upon one of the barrels in an old cider-house attached to a mouldering building in the lane. Often, too, have strange unearthly noises issued, in the dead stillness of the night, from the same building, like sounds as of a cooper's hammer wielded by no mortal hand.

The mysterious wagon survives still, someone who has lived in the village for many years recalls that in the 1950's, a girl was walking along a lane half a mile to a mile out of the village one evening when she saw a hay cart coming towards her. She was thinking about other things at the time and didn't take a lot of notice but after it had gone by, she turned round to take a look and it had disappeared. She then realised that as it had passed her, it hadn't made a sound. Jabez continues:

> The black dog has likewise been seen at Callow's Leap, a place near the foot of the Sandy Lane, on the main road side, where it is said that a mighty hunter, of the name of Callow, leaped down the precipice. A carrier, who weekly goes through the main road with a horse and cart, told me, that upon his return home one night, from Worcester to Suckley, he saw, nearly opposite to the cottage by Callow's Leap, what he took to be a man lying in the ditch; but, upon his seizing his horse's head to prevent him taking fright, he all of a sudden lost sight of the supposed human being and something like a black dog rushed close by him under the horse's neck. He also said that his horse, at two or three different times, made a dead halt at that spot, and that he had much difficulty in getting him on again. (Horses are supposed to see ghosts, even when the ghosts are invisible to their riders. Upon my once asking a countryman whether he had ever seen a ghost, he said, "No, but my horse has.")

Another haunted spot was Bate's Bush which Jabez describes as a large old maple tree standing in the middle of the cross-roads by Osebury rock. Until 1823, a suicide victim could not be buried in consecrated ground and was therefore usually interred at a cross-road with a stake driven through the heart. Jabez tells of a man named Bate who committed suicide and was said to have been buried there. The stake was from a maple tree which sprouted leaves and became a bush.

As a person by the name of William Yapp was one night, about forty years ago, returning from his father's house, situated by Alfrick Chapel, to Dodenham Hall, he had to pass by Bate's Bush; when he arrived there, the dog that accompanied him, and was a little in advance, came howling mysteriously back to him, out of the Sandy Lane. He, however, went on, but had not proceeded far before he saw something which he took to be a man without a head, leaning with his back against the steep bank on the Osebury Rock side of the lane; at which he was so frightened that he did not dare to go up to it, but hurried away home as fast as he could run.

Furthermore, says Jabez, at that same spot, a Mr Ball saw something which frightened him to death, Mr Parry saw an apparition rather like a black pig and another person was dogged by a mysterious-looking black dog-like animal.

Jabez remarks that the road from Alfrick to Lulsey was 'much more interestingly haunted'...

I have been informed by a person, that as his father, about seventy or eighty years ago, was proceeding at dead of night from Patches in Alfrick to Lulsey, he saw, as it is said others also occasionally did at the same spot, a beautiful young female figure, all in white, standing by the roadside; his horse turned suddenly round, but upon being forced back again by his rider, he started off at full gallop by the enchanting vision, and never stopped till he arrived at his journey's end.

ARLEY

The river severn runs 180 miles and has determined the development of Worcester more than any other factor. Upper Arley lies on the Severn near the Shropshire border. Apart from a few houses it has a pub, a picturesque railway station and a church containing the effigy of an unfortunate knight, Sir Walter de Bohun, who was killed in a jousting tournament on his wedding day. There was once a ferry here but this has now been replaced by a bridge.

As an enthusiastic fisherman, it was to Arley that Peter went when he took a day's holiday from his job as a glazier.

It must have been about 1980 that I went fishing at Arley. Because it was a weekday there was nobody else about. I was standing on the bank and suddenly, I realised that everything had gone very quiet. When the birds are singing you don't notice them but when they stop, you notice how deathly quiet it is. Then I saw that the river had started flowing faster and the opposite way. I looked around and I could see a bloke in a green anorak under a tree a few yards away from me on the shore. I shouted to him, 'Looks as if there's going to be a storm, mate!' but he didn't reply. I looked away for only a split second, when I turned back the bloke had disappeared. The funny thing was, he couldn't possibly have gone anywhere in that short time. The wind started to howl, the trees were bent right over and the water started running rough. It was quite frightening. I thought 'I'm getting out of here' so I went over to the pub on the other side of the river, The Harbour, and had a drink.

At that time I worked for the Council. I told my mates about it but they didn't believe me. A few weeks later, one of them said to me, 'Was that your story about Arley in the *Black Country Bugle?*'. I told him that it wasn't; he showed it to me and evidently somebody else had had a similar experience. They believed me then!

The Harbour, Arley

ASTWOOD BANK

Astwood Bank straggles along a prehistoric ridgeway running along the western edge of the Arrow Valley. Thousands of years ago great herds of bison and wild deer, together with groups of nomadic man, would have wandered where the road and ribbon development now runs. The village is just within the boundary of Feckenham Forest and the name is thought to be a corruption of East Wood Bank.

Into this busy little village came John Jukes early in the April of 1987, to a Victorian house not far from the Red Lion.

My new wife and I were looking for somewhere to live and we read this advertisement in the *Redditch Advertiser* for a couple of lodgers. I had two children from my previous marriage, a boy and a girl, aged 6 and 7 years respectively, who came to stay with me for a weekend once a fortnight.

We had a look round and we liked the house, it seemed very pleasant. We also liked the landlord, a young man in his mid twenties, very friendly. His life style was such that we saw very little of him, he went camping and hill-walking a lot. A few days after we moved in, it transpired that I had worked with the landlord's father for four years. Things were comfortable and we were very happy.

On the bank holiday at the beginning of May I went into the bathroom. It was an old-fashioned terraced house and the bathroom had been added on to the kitchen. I was washing my hands when my new wife came and put her hand on my shoulder, gave me a little kiss on the back of my neck and sighed into my ear. I felt her breath on my neck. I continued to wash my hands, I put the flannel down, dried my hands but still did n't turn round. Then I looked back, expecting to see my wife but nobody was there. The bathroom door was open and I could see through the kitchen, which was about fifteen feet long and very narrow, into the living room where my wife was sitting, watching the TV. There was no way she could have got back there so quickly. The hairs on the back of my neck began to prickle.

I remained calm. I'm quite open to the idea of spirits/ghosts because my family are often discussing them and I have been brought up in the idea that to see a spirit is a unique experience. I walked back to the living room area and said, 'That wasn't you then was it?'.

My wife answered, 'What do you mean?'. 'You just kissed me on the back of my neck'. My wife replied, 'You were in here a second ago and you said *hullo* to me'. We came to the conclusion that something strange was going on.

We didn't talk about this again until a week later, when I saw the first visual sign. We were in bed and it was early in the morning about 6 o'clock. I was the only person in the house awake when I realised that there was somebody else in the bedroom, probably at the foot of the bed. The strange thing was that if you looked directly ahead you couldn't see anything but if you kept your head still and looked to the right there was somebody there – a shadowy figure, half transparent, female, age – mid-thirties; almost average build, quite thin, about size 12, I would say in height about 5' 7". A vague shape of a dark brown dress, almost black, nearly touched the ground but was elevated about 2" from the floor. The dress had a square collar also dark brown and the collar was as if a doily had been dropped over her head, with a round piece cut out for her neck. She had long blonde hair tightly tied back in a bunch in a severe way. I couldn't see her face but I could see her hair at the back of her face.

I was not particularly worried and as I wanted to go off to sleep and the daylight was streaming in, also I was competing with the dawn chorus, I got out of bed and pulled the curtains together. The woman then disappeared. Later, I described to my wife what I had seen and she said that she had also seen this same lady. She thought it might be the ghost of a relative of hers who had died a few years previously and she was very frightened.

We were both working so you try to put these things behind you and go to work. Life was fairly normal for a week except that we both had this completely irrational feeling that somebody was there. It became more and more obvious, then she began to appear to us again. We were both seeing her and as time went on, she appeared more and more often and details were beginning to be visible. We could see that she didn't have feet but when she moved to follow us she definitely walked and didn't float or glide. There was more definition about her clothing, she wore an A-shaped dress and long sleeves which half covered her hands. The only way that I can describe her face is to say, imagine taking a photograph and tracing the outline of the features on tracing paper. We could just see that outline with the hair behind.

We noticed that she started to make appearances when we were tidying up and doing housework. She seemed to be looking over our shoulders to make sure that we did it properly. You could very rarely see her when you looked direct. For example, you would be watching TV and you would look to the right and you could see her. She was usually very busy and would move on.

By the middle of May we knew that something strange was going on. My wife was scared and I was exhilarated. Then, on 1st June we decided to mention this to the landlord. As soon as I said the house was haunted, he panicked. At first he said that he didn't want to talk about it but eventually, he admitted that his bedroom was haunted by a lady and he gave the same description. He added that he was constantly being woken up in the middle of the night being strangled by her.

I said that I hadn't found anything particularly frightening about her and she didn't seem to be angry. I suggested that it was his own fear and negative attitude, mixed with his dreams, that gave him this impression. However, at this point I did start to become a bit concerned. Fortunately, I work with someone who is a member of the Spiritualist church so I discussed this with him and asked what he would recommend, as this was not in my usual range of experiences. He told me to talk to her, he said that maybe something was bothering her.

My next encounter with her was in the bathroom where the landlord had added an en suite shower. I was showering and she joined me, she stood there fully-clothed. I said, 'I don't care who you are, this is a private thing and would you please go away!'. Off she went and we didn't see anything again for another four or five days.

One night, about two months after we had moved in, we heard the landlord shouting and screaming. From then on he refused to sleep in the attic and moved downstairs to sleep. A short time later he went to live with his parents. He was extremely worried and nervous. As far as he was concerned, ghosts were terrifying, so he left the house.

By now things were becoming quite strange to say the least. We had numerous occasions where the taps were turned on and off and the electric kettle switched on. One night, the landlord had returned to visit us and was sitting on the settee with my wife, when both taps started running in the kitchen. I said, 'This is ridiculous, I have got to see what's going on!' and I went into the kitchen. I could just see the bottom half of the woman, the top half of her body had disappeared into the kitchen unit. She appeared to be washing up which was ridiculous as the sink was ten feet away. She didn't know I was there and I stood and watched her for a good minute. She appeared to be washing up some plates, she then dried them and put them on to what was the cooker. I went back into the living room and reported what I had seen to my wife and the landlord. He got panicky and asked me to show him where she had been washing up. He told me that when he bought the house five years earlier that was where the sink used to be and he had put new kitchen units in. Now, I hadn't known that. For the first time ever I had the hairs on the back of my neck standing up. At this point I started to get very worried.

My wife and I were looking for somewhere else to live, not because of the entity but because we wanted a house of our own. A few weeks later we bought our own place and moved in.

When we moved into the house the children came to visit. My daughter by then was eight. As I tucked her up in bed , she said, 'I do like it here because there aren't any ghosts and I do hope that lady won't come to visit me at night'. I asked her what she meant and she said that when she came to stay in Astwood Bank this lady used to come to her bedroom all the time and it scared her. We told her that she had probably dreamed it.

There is a strange sequel to this story, which, I must emphasise, is not a personal experience but just hearsay. The guy that owned the house moved out. He took his girlfriend round to visit and when he went into his bedroom in the attic there was a crow trapped in there. As he opened the door it flew out between him and his girlfriend, down the stairs and out through the front door.

Shortly afterwards he sold the house.†

†John's wife, Brenda, has helped with the narrative by an occasional correction and some prompting.

BEOLEY

Between the foot of Beoley Hill
And Beoley's peal of bells,
In certain seasons of the year
An evil spirit dwells.
Its body's under four crossroads;
Its soul lies lower still;
Save when releas'd from 'lotted terms,
And then it haunts the hill.†

QUESTION OFTEN ASKED is, which is the most haunted place in Worcestershire? Many a village and even the occasional hill or river, has laid claim to this title. However, the title must surely go to Beoley, a quiet country village situated a mile to the north of the Bordesley Abbey meadows. More ghosts have come from Beoley than any other part of Worcestershire. Sightings have occurred at Beoley vicarage, Chapel Farm, Beoley Hall and Dagnall End farm, and in addition Beoley cross-roads seem to have a number of apparitions.

Beoley has had a long and eventful history. Across the road from the church is a huge mound, thought to be a hill fort, which could be as old as 1,500 BC although it has never been excavated. The church still has some Norman remnants and holds the tombs of the Sheldon family. This beautiful, holy place was was once used as a den in which to make counterfeit money, probably sometime in the eighteenth century. Finally, a murder occurred at Beoley in 1885 which shocked the country. The first police constable ever to be murdered while on duty, Police Constable James Davies, was killed by an itinerant, Moses Shrimpton, whom he had probably caught poaching.

As for ghosts and spirits, there are many old tales – of the Beoley goblin who plagued the horses as they toiled up the hill, of a charcoal burner who was suffocated by his fumes and whose crackling fire can still be heard on still dark nights, of death tokens and of phantom horses and carts. In the middle of the last century, the vicar of Beoley decided to raise money by taking the public on escorted tours of the Sheldon vaults. Afterwards he was so certain that he was being haunted by a member of the Sheldon family that he paid a man to sleep at the bottom of his

†Introduction to poem written about 1865, James Woodward.

bed at night. In 1969, two painters and decorators were working in the vicarage when they heard a woman ask them a question, they turned round to see a 'lady in old-fashioned clothing'. While they stood there, 'gob smacked', she faded away.

The mad monk

Another curious local legend is that Chapel Farm was once burned down by a mad monk. The farm took its name from one of the rooms in the house which was used as a Catholic chapel and has now been converted into a bedroom.

The present owner, Mrs Proctor, says that many people can feel a definite presence, and when the midwife arrived to deliver her first baby, she said, 'Of course, you know you have a ghost here!' Mrs Proctor has never seen the ghost herself but there is a record of it in the *Victorian William Avery Memorial Volumes.*†

> One Christmas Day, Mrs —, a Catholic, who had been on a visit to us, went up into the Chapel-room to put on her things to go home, when she heard a rustling on the floor, as of leaves in the Autumn; looking up, she saw the Priest; he disappeared near the place where the Font had formerly been. (At another time) M— was in her bed in the Chapel-room and she heard the same rustling noise, and saw the Priest – his hands stretched out is if blessing her. He had on the back of his Vestment a Lamb; he disappeared at the Font. She never was the least alarmed at anything she saw, because the things she saw looked good and happy.

Squatters

To the north of Beoley Church, hidden behind the trees, is Beoley Hall. The Sheldons were at one time one of the three richest families in England and the Hall, which was built for them, is suitably imposing. It is said that the Sheldons burned down the previous house during the civil war, sometime in the middle of the 1600s, so that it would not fall into the hands of the Parliamentarians. This may be so because most of the present house, with its elegant porch and Tuscan columns, was built about fifty years later.

In about 1780 the Sheldon's leased the house to a retired pirate (a respectable occupation in those days) and from then on there was a long history of squabbles

†Notes and Queries, number 220.

over the ownership. In 1840 the descendants of the Sheldons twice tried to take
the house by force, the first time they were let off with a reprimand but the second
time the local Steward and his posse held the heads of the seven young men under
the water of Beoley pool until they almost drowned.

Beoley Hall

In 1967 Mrs Railer and her daughter purchased the hall and Miss Railer is still
in residence.

She emphasises that although she has lived there all these years she has never
heard or seen anything strange – except once, on one cold winter's night.

The orangery was on the eastern side of the hall but in 1970 my mother
and I had to have it converted into half-a-dozen houses in order to finance
extensive repairs to the hall. I have been told that it was once the stabling
block and coach house for eighteen horses but it contains a fireplace dated
1546 and could, therefore, stand on the site of an earlier house. Under the
stucco in one of the houses are the original arches and we wonder if this
was once a Sheldon chapel.

In the January of 1970 all the houses had been sold and the residents
were due to move in the following day. My mother and I had had to move
out of the hall because of the repairs, which included the fumigation of dry

rot, and we were living temporarily in the end house nearest the drive.

It was three o'clock in the morning on a bright, moonlit night. At that time we had three dogs and they suddenly started to make a heck of a row. Mother got up and looked out of the window – the orangery is in a court-yard setting – and she saw two figures come from what was the old coach house on the side where the horses were stabled. She called to me, 'There are squatters trying to move in to an empty house, Barbara, come and look!' The reason my mother thought they were squatters was that they looked as if they were dressed in second-hand clothes from the Portabello Road. One was a girl with long brown hair and a long dark riding cape. She was with a blonde-haired chap wearing a sports suit and an Edwardian cropped jacket with narrow tweed trousers. He was looking down at her with great affection. Although my mother saw both characters, I only saw the young lady and I particularly noticed her extraordinary ram-rod posture. I did notice, too, that she had no feet but my mother was not one with whom you argued the point so I shoved my wellies on, grabbed a coat, called to the dogs and out I went. My one thought was, 'Oh Lord, we've got squat-ters in!'. Once they move in it is such a job to get them out.

I looked round but there was nobody about. Redditch New Town had not been built then so it was even quieter than it is now, in any case in those days there was no transport, people didn't have cars like they do now. I went back and told my mother nobody was there. I would mention that we hadn't had anything to drink and in any case, the dogs saw something before we did.

Well, nobody thought any more about it. I didn't particularly want to make a lot of this ghost story with new residents arriving. Then, some years later, we had a letter from an elderly lady in Worcestershire who used to visit the house a great deal. Mother had mentioned that she had seen some kind of apparition and this lady wrote back, 'I will tell you exactly what you saw' and she described these two people exactly as my mother had seen them. She also told us who they were.

Towards the end of the 19th century the house was occupied by a Mrs Kennard who was having an affair with her brother-in-law, Captain Boyd Rophfort. The letter-writer insisted that they were the parents of Lawrence of Arabia and used to visit him frequently at Oxford. She said that the case had always been kept quiet because, understandably, Mrs Kennard didn't want people to know that she had been carrying on with her brother-in-law. The young couple were recognisable by two factors, Captain Boyd had very blond hair and Mrs Kennard had a very straight posture because, when she was on the back of a horse, her father used to string her up with piano wires so that if she lost her seat they cut into her skin. This was verified by someone in the village who told me that his grandfather always used to remark that Mrs Kennard rode ramrod straight. With regard to the young lady having no feet, the level of the courtyard has been raised over the years which could explain this.

Beoley Hall has now been converted into nine apartments. Although a grade II listed building, the renovators demolished much of the interior furnishings, smashing a white marble fireplace with a Sheldon crest dated 1791and throwing the beautiful gilded carving on a bonfire.

Mystery at the crossroads†

The old Roman road, Icknield Street, runs past Beoley and, where it is crossed by the B4101 is the infamous Beoley cross-roads. These were an accident black spot last century, when carriages would overturn after going down the hill, and they continue to be accident-prone this century, with innumerable vehicle pile-ups.

Nearby was a dangerous ford, subject to sudden flooding when millers upstream opened their floodgates. In 1861 Henry Garfield was drowned here and in 1920 Mr Heath lost his son at the same place. In the 1750's Rev John Wesley, founder of the Methodist church, nearly came to grief there. No wonder the area is subject to a number of apparitions! The first cross-roads story comes from a local housewife and mother.

I've seen the ghost of Beoley cross-roads. It was over 30 years ago so there are some details which I can't recall, but the following is the little that I can remember.

It happened at a quarter-to-eightish one nasty evening in the late summer or early autumn of the mid 1950's, when it was raining slightly and the light wasn't very good. I was travelling in a van with my boyfriend and his friend, going towards Ipsley Church and away from Beoley cross-roads, near to a farmhouse and a bridge over a stream. We reached a dip in the road, and I saw, standing right in the middle of the road, a very ordinary looking man. He was facing me quite clearly and although I can't remember exactly what he was wearing I know that he appeared to be in evening dress. He was waving his right arm up and down frantically and I assumed

†Stories by Rowena, Pauline and Tony O'Neill were first publishesh in the Redditch Advertiser of 5 January 1994.

he was flagging down our van. I expected my boyfriend to put on the brakes but he didn't. I thought we were going to hit him and I shouted, 'Stop!'. My boyfriend then braked sharply and the man gave an enormous jump sideways into the hedge on his left.

I said to my boyfriend, 'Didn't you see him?' 'See what?' asked my boyfriend, 'Oh, come on', I replied, 'That man standing in the middle of the road'. Apparently, neither my boyfriend nor his friend had seen the man. They got out of the van and looked up and down the hedgerows but nothing was there. Later, I realised that his sideways jump was physically impossible.

I was so frightened that my boyfriend had to take me home. My grandmother said that I was not the first person to see an apparition along there, and I wouldn't be the last.

Her grandmother was correct. In 1972, two young ladies, Rowena and Pauline, decided to visit their local one evening. Rowena was driving.

We were going to the Village Inn so we set off towards Beoley, up past Bomfords Farm, then at the cross-roads we turned left into Icknield Street, going towards the Beoley cross-roads. It was about 7.45 in the evening and the sun was just beginning to set, so halfway down Icknield Street I switched my lights on full. Then suddenly, I said to Pauline – and she said to me at the same time – 'What's that silly devil doing in the road?' In front of us, with his back towards us, was a tall, thin man in a long cape coat, the cape part of which came to immediately below the shoulders, and a deer-stalker hat. He didn't move over to the side of the road as a normal person would but just suddenly vanished into thin air. Pauline and I could not believe it. We said to each other, 'Did you see that?'

And here is Pauline's version:

There was no colour in the apparition, it was just dark grey, consequently I though his hat looked more like a policeman's helmet. He glided across the road from right to left and disappeared as he got near the hedge. We were quite shaken up. We went to the pub and had a quick drink then we went back to inspect the road to see if we could find any explanation. But there was no reason for it.

One winter's evening 14 years later, Tony O'Neill and his wife were approaching Beoley cross-roads when:

The light was just beginning to fade, I should think it was about 5.30, but we could still see quite distinctly. I had just come off the Lily Green Road bend and into the old Icknield Street and had reached the section of the road which widens into a passing place, when I saw a strange figure walking along the edge of the road with his back towards me. The figure was at least six feet tall, and, perhaps because of his height, gave the impression of being male. He was wearing what appeared at first sight to be a dark grey cagoule or trench coat which was very long and reached almost to the ground, his feet and ankles were just visible and he was wearing galoshes or wellingtons. On his head was a hood which was very pointed at the top and came down to just below his shoulders. He had a small grey and white dog with him – we could see the leash quite clearly. Both my wife and I saw him, I was surprised to see someone walking there as not many pedestrians use that road and, as I approached, I indicated that I was about to overtake, then suddenly, 'pop', he disappeared like a soap bubble.

In the autumn of 1988, Clint Longmuir had a terrifying experience:

I'm a bit nervous about this sort of thing and I try to convince myself that it didn't really happen. I try to believe that it was the way that the orange light from the halogen lamps fell on the bushes.

It happened at about 10.30 one evening. I had a girlfriend who lived on the A441 Birmingham Road and usually, it was quite a nice drive back home to Matchborough along the B4101. However, on this particular night, when I reached the bottom of the hill at Beoley cross-roads, I glanced out of the window and the light picked out the shape of a man on the left hand side of the road. He was standing right back in the bushes and looking out towards the junction. It was hard to pick anything out but he seemed to me to be wearing a flat grey checked cap and a full length drover's coat. I turned my head away for a second and when I looked back, he had gone. It was quite scary and I don't think I shall ever forget that night.

The most recently reported sighting is from Andrew Proctor and was on 15 December 1991.

I was driving back from my aunt's to my home at Beoley, through Beoley cross-roads, when I had quite a fright! I had not long passed my driving test and found it quite unnerving at the time and even more so now when I look back on it.

It was just getting dark but visibility was quite good, and as I turned at the cross-roads to go up the hill towards the church, I could see that the road was clear and no-one was about. Then suddenly, a man appeared from nowhere and walked out right in front of my car. He was tall, of average build and from the way he walked I would say that he was about fiftyish. What was strange was they he was wearing funny clothes, a long black cloak of quite heavy fabric with a hood. It really shocked me. Fortunately, I was only going slowly so that I was able to put on the brakes and stop. Although he was facing me, his face was in shadow so that I couldn't see his features. He just stood there for several seconds, evidently looking at me, and then he walked to one side which left me free to drive on. As I drove past I looked in my mirror but he had gone. I looked back but no-one was about. There's no way he could have gone round the corner that quickly.

I wondered then if I had really seen something or whether it had been my imagination and it was not until I saw a newspaper report a few weeks later saying that other people had seen an apparition at the Beoley cross-roads that it occurred to me what it might have been.

CLAINES

At the northern tip of Worcester city is Claines. When you arrive at the Old Mug House and start looking for the non-existent car parks, you realise that this is a place which time has forgotten. The yellowed clocks jostle for a place on the walls amongst the Victorian etchings and the dartboard.

The Old Mug House is next to the church and is the only public house in the country to stand on consecrated ground. The church was rebuilt in the fifteenth century and the pub was probably erected about the same time. It has such a reputation for being haunted that the landlord has frequent requests from ghost hunters asking if they can stay the night, which he has to refuse as he does not provide overnight accommodation.

Wally Trow was landlord from 1938 to 1982 but, when you ask him about the ghost, he roars with laughter and tells the following story:

> In the early 1950's we had a gravedigger by the name of Bates and late one afternoon, the day before a funeral, I noticed that a grave hadn't been dug. Bates eventually rolled up on his bike and I said to him, 'You're never going to get that grave dug in time'. He answered, 'Oh yes I will, I'll carry on digging till late tonight, then I'll sleep in the churchyard overnight and finish off as soon as it gets light in the morning'. He dug down to about three feet, then it got dark and he couldn't see any more, so he put down some straw, climbed into the grave and pulled a piece of corrugated tin over himself. Early the next morning the milkman was trotting through the churchyard to deliver his milk when he saw this hand coming out of the grave and a voice shouted, 'What time is it?'. He nearly dropped his milk with fright!

However, Mr Trow admits that he heard many an inexplicable noise and that he had problems in the cellar where his mallet, which he used to bang the taps in, was mysteriously moved about. He also recalls that 30 or 40 years ago a Curate by the name of Mr Marks had seen a white mist, which had assumed a human form, inside the church. Mr Marks was a most responsible person, he had once been secretary to Sir Winston Churchill but had decided to enter the ministry late in life.

Wally Trow's wife takes the ghost stories more seriously and describes the years that she lived there.

> The Old Mug House was a creepy place. It was dark and full of strange noises. When we lay in bed at night we could sometimes hear the glasses rattling for no reason at all. We often heard strange footsteps. Many times I heard someone go downstairs in the night so I got out of bed to see who it was but no-one was there. I remember one afternoon when I definitely heard someone go in the house and up the stairs, I rushed to the stair door and locked it. I thought, 'Well, whoever it is, I've got them now' but when Wally and I went upstairs to see who it was, no-one was there.
>
> Sometimes things went missing but with two children we didn't think much of it. I remember something strange, though, which happened over and over again. When we went to bed at night we put a plate of biscuits

on the side in case one of the children got up in the night, but they didn't
get up and some mornings the biscuits had gone. We put it down to mice
but there were never any crumbs or droppings and other bits and pieces
of food were never touched.

John Adkins has been landlord since the summer of 1989. He and his wife, Judy,
were sceptical about ghosts when they first moved but they have had so many
strange experiences that they are beginning to change their minds. John takes up
the narrative:

The first weird event happened late one Sunday afternoon, about three
months after we had moved in. The bar was closed and we were sitting
round a table in the lounge, eating a meal with about eight friends and
neighbours when suddenly, from behind the bar, came an enormous crash.
We rushed to the bar to find half-a-dozen glasses which had been kept on
a low shelf had smashed to the floor with such force that they had been
reduced to small particles like ground glass. It was so weird that our friends,
who were staying in the cottage next door, said 'We're not stopping here
any longer!', threw their luggage in their car and drove back to London.

About six weeks later it happened again. Colin, the barman, and Joanne,
a niece who was staying temporarily to help, were leaning against one end
of the bar early one evening, having a chat, when there was a loud crash.
Several glasses had fallen to the floor and were completely shattered into
such small pieces it was impossible to tell how many had been broken.
Colin and Joanne were quite amazed because there was absolutely no
reason for it, in fact Joanne was quite frightened.

From the first day that we arrived our dog, an American spaniel, began
howling and it had never howled before. Eventually we realised that he only
howls when he is in the kitchen. The flap to the cellar is in the kitchen
and it's in the cellar that many strange things have occurred.

I'm the only person to go down the cellars and one night I went down
and turned the barrels on, then I came upstairs and served a glass of cider.
Judy went to serve a second glass but no cider came out. She said, 'The
cider's run out!' and I told her that it couldn't have because I'd only just
checked the barrel. I decided I would have to go down the cellar again to
see what was wrong so down I went and checked the piping. Then I
noticed that the electric motor was switched off. I could not believe it. This
has to be turned off manually with a switch and there is no way it could
have been done by accident. The same thing happened again a few months
later, then again, a few months after that.

Only last Saturday night something weird happened in the cellar. At four o'clock in the morning the dog began howling and this set the other dog off. The next morning I went down the cellar and I could hardly believe my eyes. All round the walls of the cellar are steps called stillages which are about a foot wide and between two and three feet in length for the barrels of beer to rest on so that they are not standing on the floor. Somehow, a barrel of beer, which takes two men to lift, had managed to remove itself from the stillage, complete with pipes and other fittings, and was resting on the floor.

The most frightening incident occurred early in 1991. This convinced my that there is something spooky about this place. Judy and I were both woken up by the noise of a door opening at half-past one in the morning. Now, when you live in an old house you get used to certain noises and we knew that it was the door of the Smoking Room. It's old and heavy and first you have to turn back the heavy door handle, then drag the door open. Next the door was closed with a loud bang. The door has a heavy bolt on the corridor side and the room contains an infra-red security device so that when the door opens, the alarm is set off. We lay there, expecting the alarm to go off but nothing happened. Again the door noisily opened and closed, followed by a rest of about 15 seconds, then it happened again. Judy said to me, 'What are you going to do about it?' I said 'Nothing, I'm just stopping here where I am!'. I was petrified, although I suppose if the alarms had gone off I would have gone downstairs. In all the door opened and banged shut six times. When we got up the next morning we found that the door was still bolted. We had the security system checked and there was nothing wrong with it.

Judy added that she would not sleep in the house alone.

On the rare occasions that my husband has to go away, my son comes to stay with me. If I was here alone and the dogs began howling I just wouldn't be able to cope. Our cleaner will never work on her own, she can hear someone moving about upstairs when she knows that nobody is there. Our barman won't stay on his own either, he hears the rattling of drawers in empty rooms and the opening and closing of doors.

BEVERE

West Claines merges into Bevere and Bevere island, so called because beavers had damned the river with the result that it had turned the area into a marshland. Until recent centuries the River Severn was not neatly channelled as it is today but often spread out into lakes and marshland. Bevere island has been used twice as a refuge for Worcestershire citizens, once during the Viking raids and again in the time of the plague.

Eventually this marshland was drained and used for farming and during the 18th century a handsome farm was built on the banks of the Severn. In late 1991 an agency nurse, Linda, was asked to go to this house as a night nurse for a stroke victim. Linda slept on a single bed in the same room as her patient.

April 11th 1992, the night of the general election, is one I shall never forget.

For some time previously I had felt uneasy in the house. I did not believe in ghosts but several experiences had made me wonder if the house were haunted. I woke several times in the night with the feeling that I had heard a cupboard door, which was next to my bed, closing. I moved my bed away from the cupboard and slept with my back to it. I was also awoken by a sensation that someone had tweaked my knees.

Anyhow, this one night I was going on duty and as I turned into their drive I saw, out of the corner of my right eye, a man running sideways to escape the headlights. His curious position attracted my attention – he was leaning sideways and he seemed to float, he seemed to be above the level of the pavement. Apart from that, he looked quite ordinary. He was wearing modern clothes – a white open-necked shirt with a dark coat and trousers, his hair was receding at the front, slightly wavy and wispy at the back and he could have had a moustache. As I looked at him he threw his arms into the air and gave a horrible grimace. His features faded away and his head shone like a round moon. Then his whole body shone from head to foot as if he had a light inside him. I was terrified but I managed to drive past and on looking back I saw that he was still there. When I reached the house I behaved quite professionally and continued with my duties as if nothing had happened. I went to bed but I stayed awake all night! Next morning I asked my employer if the house was haunted. She told me that a few evenings previously there had been a frost and, the next morning when she went out of the front door she saw that there were footprints in the frost going past the front of the house which stopped suddenly for no reason.

I couldn't go back after that. I asked the agency if I could be transferred to another post.

COOKHILL

About three miles north of the Dunnington strawberry fields is the rambling village of Cookhill. At the Dunnington end was a Cistercian nunnery, in existence as long ago as the 12th century, and fragments still remain. In 1763 a house was built on the site and the fragments were converted into a chapel for the house.

This story comes from the other end of the village, from one of several houses which were recently built on agricultural land belonging to the Ragley Estate.

A young married lady was lying in bed one night when she was surprised to hear a horse coming up the road. She heard the sound of its hooves approaching her house, then she clearly heard it step over a little low wall on to their lawn. At that point the noise of the hooves became softer because of the grass. It went round the side of the house and she heard the clatter of hooves as it went on to the hard tarmac that leads to the garage.

She woke her husband up and told him that there was a horse in their garden, to which he replied something like, 'Don't be silly, there can't be, go back to sleep!'.

The next door neighbours had a horse and she was worried that it had got out. First thing in the morning she rushed round next door and told them what she had heard. The husband said that it couldn't be their horse because it was sick and in a veterinary hospital.

She examined the lawn, expecting to find hoof marks, but nothing was there. She was still convinced that she had heard a horse and asked around to see if anyone had lost one but no-one had.

In the course of her enquiries she spoke to one of the old countrymen. He listened to her intently, and then remarked, 'Ah, that be Ebeneezer's mule'. She did some investigating and discovered that at the end of the last century, there was a farm not far from her house and the farmer's name really was Ebeneezer. He had a mule which he used to put in the shafts of his cart when he wanted to take his produce to Redditch. One day, the mule had a heart attack; Ebeneezer dug a big hole and buried it where it had dropped dead. What she also discovered was that the mule was buried almost at the spot where her house stands.

FECKENHAM

The enormous Feckenham Forest, which once covered 200 miles and took in 60 villages and hamlets, was named after this pretty little village, lined with black and white Elizabethan houses. The forest belonged to the king and his hunting lodge was here during the 12th and 13th centuries.

Feckenham had two needle mills; the Worley Hole is the mill pound for one of them while the mill itself has been converted into a house. Neil Johnson was born in Feckenham and is the only one involved in the next story to return to his birthplace.

The Worley Hole was a great favourite with us when we were lads. It was a small, overgrown pool by Feckenham mill, a short walk from the back of the Church. It was owned by Singleton & Cole of Birmingham and they never seemed to bother if we went in it. We used to swing across on a rope or go fishing in it or we used to go tracking round the edge on our bikes.

On the evening of 3 September 1963, I went there on my bike to join my friends. I reached the pool just in time to see Roger, Frankie and Derek, who had been fishing on the far side of the pool, running towards me, so terrified that they splashed straight through the waters of the stream dividing us. They had left their fishing tackle behind which was scattered everywhere, and they ran straight past me without stopping. Then I saw a white figure about fifty or sixty feet away from me, among the bushes on the other side of the pool. It was a pure white solid human form, about five feet tall although the shape kept changing. By then it was drifting away from the hole, like a will o' the wisp, but not going too fast. I can only liken it to the puff of smoke that you sometimes get out of an exhaust. At first I thought it might be one of my friends dressed up for a lark and I began throwing stones at it but after half a minute or so, it faded away.

I met up with my friends later on the playing fields and they told me that this figure, like a white whirlwind, had been chasing them.

What particularly frightened them was that, in the winter of 1962/3, someone had committed suicide there and because of the severe weather, it was several months before the body could be recovered.

GRAFTON MANOR

A strangely similar incident occurred at Grafton Manor. This graceful Tudor manor house was originally the home of the Grafton family but came into the hands of Sir Humphrey Stafford in 1449. He was executed for treason early in the reign of Henry VII. In 1555 it passed into the hands of John Talbot, a relative of the Earl of Shrewsbury, who spent most of his life either in prison or under curfew for his religious beliefs. He managed to rebuild the house in 1567, putting the inscription over the porch door:

> *Plenty and grace bide in this place*
> *While every man is placed in his degree there is both peace and unity*
> *Solomon said there is none accord when every man would be a lord.*†

Which remains to this day, despite a severe fire in 1710. The house was extensively rebuilt in the 1860s and is now a hotel.

As an energetic young man Carl Mills is not usually interested in old mansions but the hot summer of 1995 found him lounging indoors, idly flipping through the pages of a local history book. A description of Grafton Manor caught his eye and therefore when, late one evening a few days later, he and three friends were wondering where they could go, Carl made a suggestion.

We decided to go for a midnight walk, somewhere dark, mysterious, and spooky so I suggested Grafton Manor pool. There was Clare, and two friends of ours, John and Karen. We drove to the Manor house and were able to park near to the pool.

We walked along the road until we came to the edge of the pool and saw the crossed trees where a lady is supposed to have drowned herself. John and Karen were in front as we continued walking towards the manor. We paused and were looking across to the bridge when we noticed, through a gap in the hedge on our left, a patch of fog on the bank. It was most peculiar fog and it was just in that one patch. It kept rolling off the bank and dropping into the water. Suddenly it came towards us and when it was ten or fifteen feet away it started to swirl in two spirals, perfect circles, side by side, both going in opposite directions, rather like candy floss. When it was about 10 or 15 feet away the shape began to change and it began to assume a human form. It went up and up until it was about six feet tall and at the same time it narrowed, so that it was very thin. The top part seemed to

†Modern translation.

divide into two peaks like arms. When it came to within six feet of us we decided to retreat to the car and drive back to the entrance gates.

Clare and Karen decided to stay where they were in the car but John and I wanted to take another look so we drove back to the lake. By this time the fog had gone towards the back of the lake, on the right hand side. To me it now looked as if it had formed the shape of a bandstand. I could see a flat roof and thin struts holding the roof up and I could see the shapes of people in the bandstand. There was a flat pier running from the bandstand to the bank. I stayed there but the fog seemed to be attracted by our presence and started to come towards us. When it was about ten feet away we ran back to the car again.

The next day I went back to have a look at the place and where I clearly saw the bank the previous night there was now no bank there, it was much further back.

The two girls were too frightened to talk about the experience, but John added:

We were standing there, looking across the lake when we saw this fluffy white mist coming towards us. It was about six feet tall and twirling, in two circles. As it got nearer it began to rise and go higher. At that point I ran back to the car, but I returned with Carl to take a second look. This time the mist was much larger and had settled in the middle of the lake, it was then a square shape with a triangular roof and there was something going on in the middle of the mist. When it moved towards us we went back to the car.

GREAT WITLEY

Witley Court is by far the most spectacular ruin in Worcestershire. The first Earl of Dudley purchased the house in 1837 with a fortune made from mining and transformed it into a magnificent Palladian palace. The opulence was beyond belief. One fountain alone cost £26,000. His second son was a friend of the Prince of Wales (later Edward VII) and to the house came a succession of kings, queens, dukes, duchesses – all the aristocracy of Victorian and Edwardian Europe. By the 1920's the Dudley fortune had, not surprisingly, declined and when the Countess of Dudley was drowned while swimming in Ireland , Witley Court was sold to a businessman from Kidderminster. In 1937, fire broke out and destroyed the east wing. The owner decided to sell what was left so it was divided up into separate lots and sold to demolition contractors.

Witley Court

No-one can visit such a huge, eerie, beautiful ruin without thoughts of ghosts coming to mind. Some of those living nearby claim to have heard unfamiliar noises and seen lights in windows, and this young man is among them.

I live not far from Witley Court and it's a fabulous place. When I was told about a strange sound that comes at night from the end of the curved wing, I was very keen to hear it. The problem was that I'm very nervous of that kind of thing so I decided to go first to the local pub and down a few pints, then, with all fear gone, I was ready for some friends to fetch me. Off we all went, very late in the evening, and parked at the end of the track. We crept in, and as we walked past the east wing and in front of that enormous entrance facade we could see strange lights in the windows. Then we stood there at the end of the crescent wing and we could all hear it. It was like an amplified, heavy breathing, very loud. I thought, 'At last, a ghost on call, I can go at any time in the evening with my sceptical friends and convince them that there are ghosts!'.

I spread the word and my daughter's boyfriend wanted to hear it. So down a few pints again and off we went. We pulled up outside the main gates but this time we heard a voice saying, 'What are you doing here?' and the police grabbed us. They had been lying in wait for vandals; we had some difficulty convincing them we were on an innocent errand looking for ghosts. In the end they agreed to let us go to the crescent wing providing they came with us. We all stood there and you could hear the noise as plain as day. I've never seen a couple of policemen run so quickly in all my life.

Delphine from Worcester city is one of the few to have seen some kind of apparition there.

When I was a child my two friends and I used to go out on our bikes and try and find mysterious places – we used to call that 'an adventure'. One Sunday morning in 1949 we came across this wonderful ruin. I know now that it was Witley Court. It was so impressive and so deserted that my friends said, 'I'm not going in there!' so I crawled through a hole in the fence and went in on my own. As I was wandering round I came across this conservatory place, and through the broken panes of glass I could see that it was full of geraniums, camellias and other exotic plants growing wild. The door was broken so that I was able to get inside. To my surprise there was a man in a dark blue suit at the far end watering the plants with one of those watering cans with a long spout. He seemed very old to me then but I suppose he was about 45 or 50. He had a nice, chubby face (I'm sure he had once been very handsome) and he had thick grey grizzled hair, the kind that stays with a man until he's ninety. Being a nosey child, I thought I'd go and ask him what he was doing looking after the plants when nobody lived there. As I walked towards him the sun came through the glass and the man just faded away. I just stood there, absolutely amazed.

The organisers are often appealing among local people for helpers and one morning in about 1986, a gentleman who has lived on the edge of the site for twenty years, was acting as unofficial custodian, when:

I was doing a tour of the grounds about elevenish and I was walking past the south west side when I noticed a figure sitting in the first floor window which is next but one to the Orangery. He was about 20 or 30 yards away but I saw him quite clearly, he was sitting on the inside window sill with one leg up, tucked under his chin.

Part of a custodian's job is to keep people away from the inside of the building, which is unsafe. If we see someone inside the building, our policy is not to confront them but to ask them to leave then walk away, expecting them to follow. As I walked past, I turned round and called, 'You are not allowed in, would you please move outside the fenced area!'.

I turned away and went to walk on. As I did so, I thought how peculiar this chap's dress was. He was wearing a loose-fitting jacket which was lying open, breeches that finished just below the knee and a cloth cap. He was wearing some form of leggings in a coarse fabric, like sacking. I can't remember the precise colour of his clothes but I know that brown was the predominant colour. I stopped, turned round and looked back but he was gone. Then when I thought about it, I realised that it would have taken a mountaineer to climb up to that position as there is no floor or staircase behind that window.

He must have been there for several seconds because I had time to make my speech!

A restoration committee has been established to stabilise the ruins and restore certain areas of the house. One of its first aims is to recreate the glories of the fountains and to have at least the Poseidon fountain working again.

THE HABINGTONS AND HARVINGTON HALL

ANY OF THE RESPECTABLE, law-abiding citizens who choose to retire in the quite backwaters of Worcestershire would be amazed to learn that the county has been, at times, a revolutionary hotbed. Before the 1530's, the state religion was, of course, Roman Catholic, but Henry VIII separated the religion of England from that of Rome and established his own church. Many of the rich and influential families of Worcestershire refused to give up their Roman Catholicism. For almost two hundred years they hid priests in their grand homes, said mass in secret chapels and from time to time plotted to put a Roman Catholic on the throne. A Worcestershire man was put to death for taking part in the Babington plot of 1586, the Gunpowder Plot of 1605 originated in Worcestershire and the Stuart uprising of 1715 was supported by the Knottisfords of Studley, the Throckmortons of Coughton Court and the Sheldons of Beoley.

The gunpowder plot

Among the families implicated in the Gunpowder Plot were the Lyttletons of Hagley Hall, the Wintours of Huddington Hall, the Talbots of Grafton and the Habingtons of Hindlip. Friends and relatives of the conspirators gathered at Coughton Court, home of the Throckmortons, on the evening of 5 November and there must also have been sympathisers at Lord Windsor's Hewell Grange, from where the fleeing conspirators collected fresh gunpowder. Tradition has it that the plot was hatched by the two Wintour brothers and the grey ghost of their mother still agitatedly walks up and down the upper gallery of Huddington Hall, waiting for news.

The gunpowder plot was followed by an anti-catholic purge. The Sheriff of Worcester and his posse arrived at Hindlip House, the home of Thomas Habington, an ardent Roman Catholic. They began tearing it to pieces in an attempt to find hidden priests. The house had been built by Thomas's father and was filled with a rabbit warren of hiding places so ingenious that the two priests who were in hiding were never discovered but eventually gave themselves up. They were carted away to be hung, drawn and quartered.

Thomas Habington had wisely chosen to holiday abroad when all this was taking place, nevertheless he was arrested on his return but released on condition that he never left the county. He entertained himself for the rest of his days writing a history of Worcestershire which has provided many interesting snippets

for this book. Hindlip House was rebuilt in the early 1800's and is now the Head-
quarters of the Worcestershire Constabulary.

The Babington plot

This was the second time that Thomas Habington had narrowly escaped a polit-
ical death. Nineteen years earlier, in 1586, his older brother had been sent to the
gallows for his part in the Babington Plot and Thomas had also been implicated.
The plot was a conspiracy to rescue the Roman Catholic Mary Queen of Scots,
who had been Elizabeth's prisoner for almost twenty years, and assassinate Queen
Elizabeth. The Babington Plot is important because Elizabeth then realised that
Mary would be a continual threat to the throne and she therefore gave permission for Mary to be executed.

Thomas only escaped because of his youth and the fact that he was Queen
Elizabeth's godchild. There were two reasons why Thomas should plot against
his godmother: first, he was a Catholic. Secondly, Queen Elizabeth had taken a
fancy to his tall and handsome father, whose income had proved insufficient for
the expenses of courtly living, consequently he had died young, a ruined man. No
doubt Queen Elizabeth was not popular in the Habington household.

Thomas Habington also owned part of the Manor of Woodend which lay
about three miles northwest of Worcester and had been known for centuries as
Habington's Place. Woodend farm still exists on the road from Elgar's birthplace
to Martley, to the right is a track to the main farm buildings, to the left is the
remains of the moated farmhouse. On the Worcester side of the main buildings
is an unusually shaped field elongated into a triangle. A small piece of woodland
runs round either side of this triangle and the woods are heavily fenced with no
exit or entrance. A local farmer's wife often passes this way and early one summer
evening, in about 1985, she saw a curious scene.

> I was walking along the road past this field when I heard a jingling noise,
> quite distant but very loud. I looked quickly in the direction of the noise
> and I saw, some way away, three riders in Elizabethan costume coming out
> of the woods on the left hand side of the field. I was quite fascinated, I just
> stood there, watching them. One was mainly in blue, the other in brown
> and I can't remember what colour the third was wearing but I do recall that
> they were on dark-coloured horses. They were wearing flat velvet hats with
> large feathers in them and they all had wide, white lace cuffs.
>
> They were coming away from the direction of Woodend farm, they cut
> across the field and re-entered the woods on the other side. I thought I

would like to get another look at them and I waited to see if they would come back, but the noise faded away and I never saw them again.

I have walked past the field many times since and it has occurred to me that there could have been a path across the field many years ago because further along the road is a spinney which looks as if it was once an exit place.

In *'Costume 1066 – 1966'*, the hats of 1558 – 70 are described as 'small, flat hats of silk, velvet or taffeta with feather trim' and the illustrations show that these continued to be worn up to and including 1586. Wide, white lace cuffs are also in fashion during this period.

Who were these three riders? Had the farmer's wife linked into some event which was of such importance that it had left an impression on time?

Persecuted priests

From 1678, for five years, the England of Charles II was whipped into an anti-Catholic hysteria so intense that it almost provoked a revolution. 30,000 Catholics fled to London in fear of their lives, hundreds of priests were imprisoned and over thirty of them taken to the gallows. Among them were two priests who had lived for long periods at Harvington Hall, near Chaddesley Corbett, John Kemble and John Wall.

John Wall was in charge of Harvington Hall for 12 years. He was taken prisoner at Rushock and was the last priest to be hung in England in 1679. John Kemble was seized at Pembridge Castle and is famous for his calm acceptance of his fate. Before his death he sat and smoked a last pipe with his gaolers. However, this was not the end of John Kemble, as Alan Cox, the Custodian, reports:

> In 1987, a lady having a cup of tea in the tearoom before going around the rest of the house insisted that she had seen 'an elderly man in old-fashioned clothes smoking a pipe and looking out of the restaurant window'. She apparently assumed he was a guide in costume having a tea break. We informed her that there was nobody of that appearance in the house, and she later identified the man, from a pen drawing in one of the rooms of the hall, as John Kemble.

Harvington Hall is famous for its priest's hiding places, no other building in England has so many hiding places so ingeniously devised. It is not surprising that many apparitions have been seen in this mysterious and exciting house. The *Worcester Evening News* of 10 July 1978 contains a letter by Etta Lugard who lived at Harvington Hall for 17 years.

> I took thousands of Yanks over the hall during the war. They loved it and always asked, 'Have you got a ghost?'. Yes, we had many experiences during our years of service there...
>
> We were the first curators and I often used to go up into the banqueting hall for a little music. I played on a Victorian piano (Playel) which was presented to the hall by the donor who purchased the hall in 1923 from the Throckmorton family. The incident I relate happened one evening about the middle of the 1930's, perhaps 1935 but I'm not quite certain which.
>
> One had in those days no electricity, only gas, so wishing to amuse myself I carried a small weighted lamp, known as a Kelly lamp, in my hand and placed it on a large carved table which stood in the middle of the room. I had been playing over some old songs which my late father loved and I often sang to him, when suddenly, I felt the chair on which I sat begin to rock gently to and fro. Then I felt hands on my shoulders, the fingers seemed to press into my collar bone. For a moment, I thought it might have been my son who was at that time perhaps 16 or 17 years old and was full of his fun. Turning quickly to catch him, as I thought, and calling out, 'Don't do that!' but there was no one there. It could not have been possible for him to get out of the room, the distance to the three doors was too great.
>
> I turned again to the piano and began again to play. In a little while the hands again grasped my shoulders and I began to feel as though I was being pushed into the instrument. I began to feel very annoyed and yet overcome with a feeling of being extinguished. I jumped up from my seat but my legs refused to support me. I looked round the shadow-filled room half expected to see something. Nothing. I began to think, 'I have to get to the table, hold the lamp and walk across the door leading to the drawing room then down a short staircase along a passage into the courtyard and across to our quarters'.
>
> I managed that eventually and remember pulling the heavy oak door to, but I don't know how I got across the courtyard, I think I flew. What became of the little brass lamp we never know, it was never seen again'.

An Edwardian schoolmistress is said to occasionally put in an appearance and Alan Cox has recorded an incident which occurred in 1988.

A visitor to the hall, on entering one of the bedrooms said she saw 'a lady in Edwardian dress sitting in the corner of the room'. The room she entered was occupied, in the early years of this century, by a schoolmistress who taught in the village school at the end of the garden.

At the beginning of the 1992 season, two residents had an unnerving experience. A group of historical re-enactors arrived to stay overnight in the house, amongst them Adrian Durkin who was then working on the archaeological project at Dudley Castle, and who writes:

During the re-enactment, it was necessary for those taking part to stay overnight in the house and I occupied one of the upstairs rooms next door to another room where two colleagues were sleeping. My room was the end one of three and the two colleagues were sleeping in the second room. The third room at the far end had a door into the second room which was locked with a padlock.

During the night, the two re-enactors sleeping in the middle room were awakened. Neither was aware that the other was awake but each had become aware of a presence which could not be defined. It was not a figure but seemed to be an entity of darkness that left the locked room through the padlocked door, crossed the room where they were sleeping and went into the corridor which ran alongside all three rooms. At this, one of the two re-enactors sprang up and tried the door, only to find it still securely locked. The two now terrified men did not sleep a wink for the rest of the night.

As soon as it became light they left the room and subsequently told their story to their colleagues. There was much hilarity and reference to spirits other than the ethereal variety. The narrator of this tale who, you remember, was sleeping in the room next door, slept through the entire incident and did not see a thing.

To quote Hamlet, 'There are more things in heaven and earth... Than are dreamt of in your philosophy', and mysterious though these hauntings may be, there is an even stranger sequel. John Kemble's hand was removed after his execution and kept as a relic at the church of St Francis Xavier in Hereford. The *Worcestershire Evening News* of 20 July 1995 devoted half a page to the fact that the relic appeared to have brought about a remarkable recovery. A certain Father Jenkins had been seriously ill in hospital after a heart attack, doctors having given up hope, when a friend brought the hand to his bedside. The priest almost immediately began to improve and by the edition dated 25 July was talking about returning to his parish.

HANBURY

The farmland of Hanbury rises to a grassy peak on which stands the old parish church of Saint Mary's. The village is almost two miles away; one of its most interesting buildings is St Mark's Chapel of Ease, which has now been converted into a forge, a dramatic fusion of heat and cold, light and darkness, noise and silence. Every surface – wall, floor and ceiling, is crammed with coal-black glistening fragments of wrought iron. The forge has been owned and worked by Mr Knight since 1975, who is certain that it has some kind of presence.

I can feel it. When I'm working late, sitting at the bench, I can feel a coldness at the back of me, as if someone is there, I turn round but there's no-one to be seen. I'm sure this presence is a friendly one and I'm not afraid of it, but it's very mischievous. I put tools out for a job the night before and when I arrive the next morning, they've gone. Then a day or two later there they are exactly where we left them. The last thing that went missing was a photograph of a bronze jug I was making for a church at Stourport. I left it on the bench and overnight it disappeared. I searched the place for it and I couldn't find it, then two days later it was back on the bench exactly where I thought I had left it.

I often wonder if this is the ghost of Emma Vernon. She is said to haunt this area. A friend of mine saw her in about 1982. He was a bellringer at Hanbury Church and as he was responsible for locking up, he was always the last one to leave. Late one night he had just left the church when he saw, by the light of the moon, this whitey-grey figure come up the path towards the church and disappear through the door which he had just locked. It scared him out of his wits. The next morning he came to me and said, 'I've seen Emma Vernon'.

The Country Girl public house is on the edge of the Hanbury beech woods. Late one afternoon in 1983, a young man sat in his car in the car park, waiting for his girlfriend to finish her duties for the day in the kitchens. At the rear of the car park is a small pool, and as he waited, he saw a white, misty shape rise slowly out of the water. He later described it as a 'human-shaped cloud of white fog – it stayed in one place and didn't move about'. Pale and shaking, he shot out of his car and into the kitchen where he had to sit in a chair for twenty minutes until he had recovered. Local people said that he had seen the ghost of Emma Vernon which was seen so many times during the 1970's and 80's that it became quite a tourist attraction.

The heiress and the curate

Hanbury Hall

Emma Vernon lived at Hanbury Hall and was the great-granddaughter of Sir Thomas Vernon, a distinguished barrister who built the hall in 1710. He still reclines in full regalia on his monument in Hanbury Church. Emma was an only child and in 1776, when she was 21, she was married to Henry Cecil of an old and distinguished family. When Emma had only been married for three years she eloped with the local curate, William Sneyd. Henry Cecil knew that he would be the laughing stock of London so he changed his name to John Jones and buried himself in Shropshire. There he bigamously married a farmer's daughter, Sarah Hoggins. He later inherited the title, Marquise of Exeter, and poor Sarah found herself entrenched in high society as a Countess. Her dilemma fired the imagination of poets (even Alfred Tennyson wrote 12 stanzas about her), musicians (including an oratorio which was composed in her honour) and writers (she has been the heroine of at least two books). As for Emma Vernon, her beloved curate died of consumption in Portugal and she returned to Hanbury, but the house now belonged to her husband and the contents had been sold to pay for the divorce. She turned to a local solicitor at Henley-in Arden, John Phillips, to sort out her affairs which were partly solved by their marriage twelve months later. However, Emma's curate was always her greatest love and when she lay dying she sent for someone who had once been her maid and asked her to make sure that she was buried wrapped in the blanket in which she had nursed her dying curate.

Emma was buried at her own request in unconsecrated ground and her tomb, recently renovated, still remains on the edge of St Mary's church yard, while her spirit wanders free in the woods and meadows of Hanbury.

KEMPSEY

Kempsey village straggles along the A38, about five miles south of Worcester, where the road runs close to a curve in the River Severn. It makes the claim of being one of the oldest villages in Worcestershire, having iron age, Saxon, Roman and Norman associations. A magnificent Bishop's palace once stood here but it has now completely disappeared.

The following is one of those fascinating and inexplicable occasions when two people see the same apparition. Jane tells her story first.

At the beginning of winter 1994, my friend, Tracey, and her husband came up from Bath for a weekend, and as they arrived quite late we had hung on to walk our dogs. However, my husband and hers decided they didn't wish to accompany us on the walk so she and I set off by ourselves. We headed down Pixham Ferry Lane which leads to the ham where at one time a ferry used to cross the Severn. The lane is crossed at one point by Old Road South and when we reached these cross roads we turned right to carry on along Old Road South. It was a typical clear, bright autumnal night and as we walked we were laughing and chatting and engrossed in conversation.

Suddenly, I noticed a man leaning against the farm gate with his legs crossed. He was about thirty-five with dark hair and he looked like a Victorian farm labourer with a neckerchief, hob-nailed boots, a cap set at a cockey angle and the cheekiest grin you ever saw. I saw him quite distinctly, he looked perfectly real. Both my friend and I caught our breath, took several steps back, looked at each other and looked back at the figure but he had gone. Had he stayed a bit longer I feel sure he would have said, 'Evenin' ladies!'

Tracey's version differs slightly.

It was in the late Autumn, we had come up to Kempsey for a weekend visit. As neither of our husbands wanted to walk the dogs and it was getting late (about 11.30 pm), we decided to go on our own. It was a cold, crisp night, the moon was up, the stars were out, and we could see everything very clearly.

Suddenly, I had this prickly feeling, as if I was being watched. I then saw, leaning back against a gate leading into a field, the black shape of a human figure, or to describe it more accurately, a black void which was blocking out everything behind it. I felt that it was looking up the lane as we came down, and as we walked past I felt that he was watching us go down the lane.

KIDDERMINSTER NORTH

A few miles north of Kidderminster is an old-established dairy farm. The farm-house was rebuilt between the wars and is of red brick, solid and unpretentious but roomy and comfortable. This is not at all the type of building to harbour a ghost, however, mysterious foundations lie beneath its walls, as Mrs West* explains.

I don't know why she should haunt this house, it's just a red brick farm-house although the cellars are older, so are the barns, and there are the foundations of other buildings by the side of the house. I have heard that the people who originally built in this area were allowed to do so on condition that they built a chapel. There must therefore have been a chapel here but no-one knows where it was. I often wonder if the enormous cornerstone just outside the farmhouse was anything to do with it.

My husband's family has lived in this house since 1930. Before that the family who lived here thought the house was haunted, nobody knows by what or by whom. We call her the green lady. I don't know why this is, apart from knowing she's a lady – I haven't ever seen her wearing green.

Various people who have lived and stayed here have heard and seen different things. There is a row of bells in the passage and the bells have rung by themselves – my husband has heard them but I haven't.

Nobody uses our front door because we have a farmyard. Everyone parks in the yard and uses the back door. The front hall is stone-flagged and the door is difficult to open, you have to drag it over the flagstones. Because no-one will sleep in the room above the hall, I use it as a study. I was working in there one evening when my husband called that he was going out to the local and at 9.50 I heard him walk through the house, go out the back and drive away. Ten minutes later I went downstairs and the front door was wide open. In those ten minutes the door had opened noiselessly all by itself. I thought someone had broken in so I cautiously did a tour of the house. When my husband came home I asked him if he had gone out of the front door and he said that of course he hadn't and he was certain it was closed when he left.

When my sister stayed overnight, she slept in a room over the front hall. The next morning, she said that she had heard sounds in the wall. I said that it was impossible, the wall is of solid brick. My son said she was right, he had heard them too when he slept in that room. My husband agreed with them and he described the noise as somebody rustling a crisp packet. All three of them were therefore aware of these noises but they hadn't told each other beforehand so it wasn't auto-suggestion.

When my son was small he used to sleep in this room. One night, I carried him upstairs and when we reached the room he clung to me and said, 'Who's that in my room?'. Then I put the light on and he said, 'Oh yes, nobody's there!'. My grandson sleeps in there once a month when he comes to stay. Recently, when he got back home someone said to him, 'Did you have a nice time?' and he said, 'Not really, there was a lady in my room who kept calling my name'. My son's friend slept there overnight and the following morning he said to my son, 'What was your mother doing in my room in the middle of the night?'.

The first floor has a long corridor with doors off each side. I was sitting in my study with my daughter in the bathroom and my son in his bedroom when I heard him call out, 'What is it?'. I called, 'Did you call?" and his reply was, 'Did you want anything?'". Apparently, someone had knocked on his door. I said that he must have been mistaken but my daughter put her head out of the bathroom and said that she had heard the knocking too. We thought it could have been my husband making a noise, putting the bottles out or something, but it wasn't him. It didn't frighten us, it was a very fleeting thing.

There was one lady staying here with her child and she came rushing down the stairs and said something had been standing behind her. She had rushed out of the room leaving the child behind!

My brother-in-law went into the dairy one evening to cut himself something to eat. He saw somebody standing there which frightened him so much that he went without his supper.

I saw something once but it was just a shape, I couldn't even say that it had human form. We have a big farmhouse kitchen and a parlour linked by a glass panel door. I was alone in the house one evening, cooking a meal. I turned round to the table – the parlour was in darkness – and I saw something in there. It was just a grey shape, and was definitely not my reflection. It just disappeared. I was quite frightened.

I went to bed one night and I switched off the light. I heard my husband come upstairs and I felt his weight on my side of the bed as he sat down. I wondered why he had decided to sit on my side of the bed and not his own and I asked, 'What's the matter?' There was no reply. Again I asked him what the matter was and again there was no reply. I felt the weight go from the bed as he stood up. I reached for the light cord, switched on the light and no-one was there.

There was one very sinister thing that frightened me quite badly. My son's marriage had broken up and he was living back here. I went into the bedroom to make his bed and I was suddenly aware that the light cord was swinging. I had the totally irrational thought that the cord was dangerous and could swing round someone's neck. I came out of the room and shut the door. The next day my son said to me, 'Was that your idea of a joke?' I asked him what he meant. He said that when he reached up to switch off the light he had found the cord tied in a hangman's noose. For a few days I wouldn't let my daughter stay here, I felt that the house was evil.

I have sometimes wondered if the strange things that happen here are connected with emotional upheavals. When the occurrances were at their worst, my son's marriage had broken up and my grandson was very upset. We're over that now, our house is a happy one again and the incidents have died down.

The dogs have never been willing to go into the cellar which is very strange because they will usually go anywhere. Down there is a passage-way which seems to have a hollow sound at the end. One of my grand-daughters is in New Zealand and she asked me to draw a plan of the house. I measured the first floor and the ground floor but when I came to the cellars they don't go the length of the house and they stop just under the room with the noises in the wall. I have often wondered if this is significant, especially when I found large sandstone foundations just outside the house. I thought there might be a possibility that the chapel had been sited here.

Our ghost is nothing very dramatic. It's simply part of our lives. We just take it for granted and we rarely talk about it. It doesn't seem very impor-tant or very interesting to me. Just occasionally, disturbing things happen which we can't explain, then we do have a feeling of disquiet but it's very fleeting. We all like living here, it's a nice peaceful atmosphere.

KINGTON

Towards the end of June in 1348, two merchant ships arrived in Weymouth, bring-ing with them unimaginable disaster in the form of the Black Death – bubonic plague. By the time the ravages of this first plague had died down a year later, more than a million people (a third of the population) had perished. Over a thousand villages had been deserted, one of which was at Kington, between Redditch and Worcester, where the heavy undulations of the streets and foundations can still be seen in one of the fields. A young couple with a small daughter have recently moved into a farmhouse nearby.

This is our fourth house and we've never had any trouble in any of the other houses. We moved here about three years ago, although the house is 18th century it could be built on the site of an older house.

We haven't get a headless horseman or anything like that but we have had a series of events which have puzzled us, to say the least. We seem to have a bit of a pattern of someone who has a passion for stroking brows and sitting on legs. It mainly seems to be on the middle and the top floor and it's bedroom-related.

Not long after we moved in, I was in the bathroom with my daughter who was then aged six and my wife was downstairs, when my daughter looked to the open doorway and said, 'Was that mummy who went past then?'. I said that I knew her mother was downstairs and she answered, 'Well, who was that lady who has just gone past?'. We didn't want to frighten her so we simply passed this off.

A month or two later I was in the bathroom again, this time alone and drying myself, when I heard the sound of a crinoline behind me. Now, I don't know anything about clothing but I can tell you that that was a crinoline. The hairs on the back of my head went 'whoosh!'. Even now it makes the hairs on my head stand up just to think about it. Since then we have called it 'she' or 'my lady'.

Now, I'm a very heavy sleeper. Sadam Hussein could wake me up and I'd just say, 'Oh, shush!' and go back to sleep again. However, one night I was woken up by this sensation of having my forehead felt. Someone seemed to be reaching over from the back of my head and putting four fingers on my forehead.

When I woke up I rather disregarded this – you don't know whether or not you've imagined these things – and I didn't tell anyone. Four months later the in-laws were staying with us. My father-in-law had exactly the same experience. However, as well as the fingers he felt a dead weight on his legs so that he was unable to move, as if something was sitting on him. I didn't know about my father-in-law's experience until he mentioned it to my wife, and he hadn't known about mine.

On New Year's Eve, to bring in 1995, we had a party here with about twelve or fifteen guests. My wife and I were in the lounge, she was just about two feet in from the lounge door and I was further inside about a yard in front of her. I can't remember what was going on at the party. Suddenly I felt something brush against the back of my calf, a very definite feeling. I turned round to see what was there to find my wife was doing exactly the same. She turned back and our eyes met. It was so remarkable that one of our friends who was in the room observed us and it was clear to him that something was going on. He came and asked us what it was and was very interested in our reply.

Three weeks ago my wife felt something tugging her undersheet – the sheet on which she was lying – and nearly pulling her out of bed. A couple of days ago she had the sensation of passing someone on the stairs.

About a month ago I mentioned this to one of our neighbours. Through various friends he knew the son of the man who lived here and died in the house four or five years ago. The son said that towards the end he was delirious and he thought that his mother was stroking his brow. A few days later he had recovered slightly and was rather more compos mentis. He said then that his wife had been sitting and bathing his brow when she hadn't.

Afterwards, we wonder if we've been imagining it. We're new to this business. We've never had anything like it before.

LEIGH

The tiny village of Leigh lies on the river Teme, equidistant from Worcester and Great Malvern. The Church, St Eadburga, has a great treasure; an exquisite, four feet high stone statue of Christ which is nearly 800 years old. Better known is the great barn at Leigh Court, the longest medieval barn and the largest cruck building in the county. The original Leigh Court has disappeared and the present building is a late sixteenth century house of brick.

Jabez Allies devotes several pages to Leigh. He tells of Edmund Colles, a grave and learned justice of the shire but whose grandson of the same name was forced to sell the manor of Leigh in the first half of the seventeeth century because of his debts.

I well remember, in my juvenile days, hearing old people speak of a spectre that formerly appeared in the parish of Leigh... which they called, "Old Coles". They said that he frequently used, at dead of night, to ride as swift as the wind down that part of the public road between Bransford and Brocamin, called Leigh Walk, in a coach drawn by four horses, with fire flying out of their nostrils; and that they invariably dashed right over the great barn at Leigh Court and then on into the river Teme. It was likewise said, that this perturbed spirit was at length laid in a neighbouring pool by twelve parsons, at dead of night, by the light of an inch of candle; and, as he was not to rise again until the candle was quite burnt out, it was, therefore, thrown into the pool, and to make all sure the pool was filled up...

A more macabre story of Edmund Colles the younger exists among the local legends. In an attempt to improve his finances, he disguised himself as a highwayman and waylaid a horse-riding friend, said to be John Leitchcroft, a farmer at Brocamin, about a mile away. Evidently he under-estimated his friend's ability as a swordsman because, quick as a flash, John whipped out his sword and lashed out at the highwayman. John galloped home but when he went to unsaddle his horse, he was appalled to find a severed hand still clutching bridle, and even more horrified to find it wearing a signet ring belonging to Edmund Colles. With great haste, the friend rushed to Leigh Court where he found Edmund dying from his wound. The friend forgave him and did all he could to staunch the bleeding but was unable to save Colles' life.

If this is true, then it is the origin of a story which has gone winging its way round the world since the eighteenth century. Barrie Roberts, the Walsall author, has traced its development from coaches and highwaymen, through the 1960's when a severed finger was that of a delinquent caught in the bumper of a mini, through to the 1980's when the severed hand was on a new car belonging to an unfortunate production line worker.

The final word on Leigh comes again from Jabez:

Before leaving Leigh Court, it may as well be observed that strange tales have been told of a mysterious looking crow or raven, which sometimes used to be seen at night sitting on one of the barrels in a detached cyder house, and who, with a horrid flapping of his wings, would "dout" the candle of an intruder and drive him back to the upper regions...

Probably these scarecrows were, in the good old times, almost as effective in guarding the cellars against all but the initiated, as Chubb's locks now are.

SHELSEY WALSH

For four days a year, Shelsey Walsh is bursting with crowds and noise. The world's oldest motoring Speed Event, established in 1905, is still held annually on the hillside.

Less well known is its reputation for ghosts. Tradition has it that many witches were burned at the stake in the Witchery Hole, a dingle of coppice wood. Jabez Allies comments:

> I recollect, when a boy, hearing the peasantry of Alfrick say, whenever a violent storm blew from the north, "The wind comes from Witcherly Hole:" meaning, thereby, that the broomstick hags, mounted on their aerial steeds, were then rushing southward from their mysterious hole, and were followed in their course by an atmospheric hurly-burly.

It has been estimated that between 1484 and 1782 over 300,000 witches were put to death across Europe. Witches were believed to cause death, disease or injury to cattle or mankind by spells or potions, to raise storms, to predict future events, to travel through the air on a broomstick or to transform themselves into animals. This belief in the supernatural powers of witches existed as late as the early 1800s. John Spooner of Hopton Court at Leigh kept a pack of hounds and every time the hunt went in a certain direction, these hounds would always run to Dame Cofield's cottage in Cradley. John Spooner was convinced that she was bewitching them.

Jabez also quotes a story from *The Rambler in Worcestershire* (1851) concerning Lady Lightfoot of the Court House in Little Shelsey, who is reputed to have been imprisoned and murdered by her husband.

> The people say the house is haunted, and that a Lady Lightfoot, who was imprisoned and murdered in the house, comes at night and drives a carriage and four fiery horses round some old rooms that are unoccupied, and that her ladyship's screams are heard at times over the Old Court. There she has been seen to drive her team into the moat, and carriage, horses, and all, have disappeared, the water smoking like a furnace.

STOURPORT

Stourport was nothing but a solitary inn until 1776, when the Staffordshire and Worcestershire canal arrived, to join the river Severn and the river Stour at Stourport. The new terminus became the busiest inland port in the Midlands after Birmingham.

The ghostly Sergeant has featured in the local press several times (see page 132); this account is by Neil Johnson.

The Lion Hill Drill Hall in Stourport is a red-bricked Victorian building and has been, for many years, TA barracks for the Worcestershire Regiment. One hot, balmy Tuesday evening in the middle of June in 1974, three regulars from the Worcestershire regiment decided to go over to the barracks early to set the place up for training. They were three sane, sensible people: Sergeant Joe Holden, who was in the army all his life, Second Lieutenant Kevin Glavin, a regular officer in the Worcestershires, and Corporal George Loveridge, who had been wounded at Anzia. They walked in through the main door and turned to the right where a door leads into the office. As they walked into the office, they noticed that it was uncannily cold. They looked over to the desk and sitting there, opposite to them, was a sergeant 'doing his fruit', wearing an expression of great anger and shaking his fist as if they were late on parade. He was a big man in his thirties with a moustache and obviously from the first world war, in full dress with sash and pace stick, and puttees up to the knees. Joe said, 'Who the hell's that?' and as soon as he said it the apparition disappeared.

This was not the first sighting of the apparition and it was not the last. Its presence was so well-known that one soldier, when he was on duty overnight, walked round with a loaded rifle – not that a bullet would have done anything but it made him feel safer.

Another sighting was reported in the *News of the World* in the early 1980's. The army were able to identify the apparition as a sergeant who had been killed by a truck at New Street Station prior to going to the front in the first world war.

How do I know all this? Twelve months after the sighting by the three regulars, I joined the regiment and sat at that very desk at which the apparition had been seen. Various army personnel took great pleasure in relating the story to me in detail which did not please me, particularly as I occasionally had to work alone in the building late at night.

A ghostly colour sergeant who parades the Territorial Army drill hall at Stourport late at night may be a man who died 12 years ago.

For Sgt. Isaac Nunney lived for a number of years in a house adjoining the 70 year old drill hall.

"If dad came back as a ghost that's just the sort of place he'd love to be," said his daughter, Mrs Dorothy Cook, of Church Walk, Arley Kings.

Several soldiers belonging to the Mercian TA Volunteers at Stourport have reported ghostly sightings of the sergeant in recent years.

He usually turns up when a breach of discipline has been committed, say witnesses. And the sergeant just stands there and fumes.

Geroge Loveridge, aged 58, who recently retired from the company has seen the ghost.

"He was a colour sergeant dressed in 1914 period uniform," said Gerorge. "He was well built with dark hair, a tough face, bristling moustache and carried a cane.

"He didn't say anything… just stood there and appeared to be fuming."

Mrs Cook read an earlier report of the ghost in the Evening News – and immediately recognised it as a description of her father who died in 1969 at the age of 82.

"We lived in the house attached to the drill hall from December 1931, to December 1933," she explained.

"My father was in the Territorial Army for 29 years – I don't know if I believe in ghosts, but if there are such things it could well be him.

"He was a stickler for discipline and could well be keeping a special eye on soldiers using the drill hall at Stourport."

Worcester Evening News, 2nd October 1981.

WOLVERLEY (including Besford and Trimpley)

HERE IS NO OTHER VILLAGE in England like Wolverley, it has a character all of its own. Although only just over a mile from Kidderminster, it lies hidden round a bend in the road and is quite isolated. Towering over the village, perched on the cliff edge, is a huge church, hanging over the village like some giant guardian angel. The houses are huddled beneath it, crammed together by the confines of a red cliff. The cliff itself is riddled with square holes, remnants of rock houses which were inhabited until the 1950's.

Here is a romantic setting, if ever there was one, for the legend of Sir John Attewood, the king's yeoman, who lived at Wolverley well before any of the present houses were built. He went off to the holy wars as a Crusader and was captured and imprisoned by the Saracens. According to Sir John, he was rescued by an angel and awoke to find himself in a field at Trimpley, about two miles away. He was so ragged and battle-scarred that he was unrecognisable and only his beloved dog ran to greet him. Fortunately, before leaving home he had had the foresight to break a wedding ring in two so that he and his wife could have half each and he was able to persuade the servants to take his half to his wife to reveal his identity. His wife had been persuaded against her better judgement to think about remarriage and Sir John arrived home just in time to prevent this marriage taking place. A much-damaged effigy of a knight has been preserved in the church.

Coming up the hill away from the heart of the village are two impressive buildings, one each side of the Live and Let Live public house. The lower building, with its giant Gothic portico, is the Sebright School of about 1830, the upper is the elegant Georgian mansion of the Knight family dating back to 1760. The Sebright family had purchased the manor of Besford in 1572 but the 6th baronet had married the daughter of Edward Knight and the family had endowed the school in 1620. The present school buildings replaced an earlier school.

Knight's House became part of the Sebright School in 1920 when Major Knight, Chairman of the Governors, left it to the school in Trust. It was converted into a boarding house for pupils and opened by the Prime Minister, Stanley Baldwin, who was born only about five miles away at Bewdley.

William Porter was the School Foreman/Head Gardener from 1920 until the house closed in the late 1960s and he often regaled his son with the following tale:

The headmaster's secretary lived in one of the rooms at the back of the house. In the 1960's she regularly used to see a lady in period dress, who was a member of the Knight family, walk through the room and disappear through a wall. She always knew when it was going to appear because the room went very cold. She recognised the ghost from a portrait on the wall in the main hallway. She wasn't bothered, she said it was part of the general coming and going.

Wolverley

The ghost has not been seen since the Sebright school closed to boarders. The Knight House has now been converted into flats.

Besford and the ghostly boots

The Sebright family have their own ghost story. They lived at Church Farm, Besford, near Pershore as the touching memorial to Sir Edward Sebright in the local church, dated 1679, testifies. The legend is that they kept a pack of hounds, which one night kept them awake by their incessant baying. They told the kennelman to go out and quieten them and the hounds were immediately silent. However, when the family went out the next morning, there was nothing left of the kennelman but his boots. Several times since, a pair of ghostly boots have been seen at night marching across the nearby fields.

There's a sequel to this. A few years ago a skeleton was discovered near the farm – minus the feet.

The Trimpley angel

According to the old legend Sir John Attewood was taken by an angel to a field in Trimpley. An angel-like apparition seems to dwell there still. In the tiny, mock-Romanesque church, the caretaker has heard the organ playing when he knows that the church is empty, and Dorothy Bridges must be one of the very few to be concerned about an angel's (if it was an angel) flimsy clothes.

My husband and I used to do the church flowers for the first two weeks in January. He was better at arranging them than I was, so while he carried on with our main task, I used to potter around. At half-past six one January evening in the early 1980's, we collected the church key from the Gables and let ourselves in. The key is enormous, so is the lock and so is the door. The key clonks as you turn it and as you push this huge oak door it groans and squeaks, then as you close it, the door gives a bang and a shudder. We closed the door, switched on the lights and set to work. My husband busied himself in the vestry with the flowers and I said to him, 'I'll just go and check the altar flowers' so I stepped out of the vestry, up to the alter then turned round and saw this very young girl, no more than 17, sitting about five rows down from the door. As I had not heard her come in, I thought she might have left the door open but it was firmly closed.

I said to her, 'Good heavens, you did make me jump!' She said nothing but just stared, such a strange look. I said to her, 'I didn't hear you come in'. Then I thought it was rather rude of me to begin a conversation like that, so I said, 'I'm sorry if I disturbed you while you were praying'. Again, she said nothing but just looked at me.

I was a bit shocked by her appearance. Although she was a very pretty girl with white blond hair falling on her shoulders in a pageboy bob, she looked so very pale, in fact her complexion had a definite greenish hue. She didn't look real. Also, it was the middle of January and very cold, and she was wearing such flimsy clothes. I couldn't see her skirt as she was seated in the pew with her hands in her lap but the fabric of the blouse was very thin.

She must have been freezing. I said to her, 'Aren't you cold in those clothes?' She still didn't reply but just kept staring. It gives me a shiver every time I think about the way she stared. It wasn't normal at all. I thought she had probably escaped from somewhere, we do have a small residential home a short distance away.

I went back to my husband in the vestry and he said, 'Who were you talking to?' I told him that there was a young girl sitting in the church and I asked him if he had heard her come in, because it seemed to me very strange that we had not heard the door squeak and groan as it was pushed open.

When he had finished the flowers he went out of the vestry to the alter and back again. As he walked across the front of the church he nodded to her, so he saw her, too.

This time, I listened for the door. I went into the vestry from where I can clearly hear the door and when I came out again a second or two later she had gone, as noiselessly as she had arrived.

I was quite perturbed by this incident and I went to the manager of the local residential home and asked him if any of his residents answered to the description of this young girl, but none of them did. I asked round locally but no-one had seen a pretty young girl in a flimsy dress.

Mr Bridges has confirmed that he had definitely seen a person sitting there but said that he had hardly glanced at her. He remarked that it was strange that he had not heard her either arrive or depart.[†]

[†]Dorothy Bridges has since remarried and is now Dorothy Salisbury.

Raggedstone Hill, The Malverns (see page 140)

WORCESTERSHIRE HILLS

THE MAGICAL MALVERNS

HE MALVERNS HAVE ALWAYS HAD A REPUTATION for legends, mystery and magic. This impressive nine-mile range can be seen from fifteen counties and if you stand on the top of the Worcestershire Beacon, you can see three cathedrals (Gloucester, Hereford and Worcester) and the sites of six battlefields (Edgehill, Evesham, Mortimer's Cross, Shrewsbury, Tewkesbury and Worcester). A vast forest, larger than the Feckenham or the Wyre forests once stretched in all directions from its summit.

In the time of Edward the Confessor (1042 – 1066) the forest was the property of Brictric Meawe, the prince charming of his day, young, handsome and trustworthy. He was the only Saxon at court, and the king sent him on a mission to the court of Baldwin, Earl of Flanders. Here, the Earl's daughter, Matilda, fell madly in love with him. Brictric refused Matilda's amorous advances but unfortunately for him, she later married the Duke of Normandy and was crowned queen of England in 1068. 'Hell hath no fury like a woman scorned' and Matilda lost no time in appropriating Brictric's estate and throwing him into Winchester prison, where he died.

The Victorian historian, W S Symonds, has described the religious rites on the Malverns two thousand years ago.

> There was a time, men say, when Druids and Bards assembled in crowds and dressed in a strange and savage garb to worship the "Pen Awyr" or sacred mistletoe, where it grew upon an oak in the glades of Eastnor, and when the "Fires of God" were kindled upon the peaks of the Ragged Stone and Midsummer Hills and as they flashed forth into flame, two snow-white bulls were sacrificed...

Centuries later, the Malverns were famous for their wise women. Daniel Defoe wrote in the late 1600s of the 'old legend of wonders perform'd by the witches of Mauvern'. The witch of Eldersfield was supposed to summon the devil and ride to the moon.

The shadow of Raggedstone Hill

The last but one hill at the Southern end of the Malverns is Raggedstone Hill. The giant rocks are said to have been split during the persecution of Saint Dunstan in the 900's. There is, however, another legend about the Raggedstone Hill, in which the slopes and valleys are haunted by an enormous dark shape of a monk, 'tall as a church spire', said to be the shadow of Raggedstone Hill.

This beautiful area was much-loved by the Benedictines who founded two priories here, one at Great Malvern in about 1085 and a smaller one at Little Malvern in 1125. During the fifteenth century a monk from Little Malvern Priory committed a terrible sin, perhaps when he became involved in a family feud, and the local judiciary wanted to hang him. The Church, however, had its own legal system and by way of penance the monk was made to climb up Raggedstone Hill every day on his hands and knees. Before the year was out, he had died. With his last breath, he stood on the top of the hill, and spreading out his arms, he cried, 'My curse be on thee, thou Heaven blasting hill, and on those which laid this burden on me and on all that be like as they are... May thy shadow and my shadow never cease to fall upon them...'

Those upon whom the shadow of Raggedstone hill is said to have fallen and who therefore were on the receiving end of the curse, include the Prior of Malvern, who died soon afterwards; Sir John Oldcastle, a Roman Catholic priest, burned at Smithfield during the religious persecutions; and Cardinal Wolsey, who lost everything when he failed to persuade the Pope to annul Henry VIII's marriage to Catherine of Aragon. The shadow is also said to have fallen on Little Malvern Priory itself which Henry VIII dissolved less than sixty years after it had been splendidly rebuilt.

Just nanny checking

The Malvern Hill is an idyllic setting for a child to grow up in and it is not surprising that a number of independent schools have been established in the area. During the 1970's, Anna, who now lives in Banbury, went to a well-known school housed in a rambling, four-storey Georgian house in West Malvern.

When I was thirteen I was moved to a bedroom in the main house. I never liked this room and occasionally I would wake up during the night, feeling as if something were trying to choke me. Then, after almost a year, I saw a ghost there. One lunch-time, I hurried to my locker to fetch something, and there she was, standing in front of the dressing table. I thought, 'Oh my God!'. I saw her quite clearly, as if she were a real person. She was quite elderly, in her sixties, I would say, and she was wearing the old-fashioned black uniform of a nanny with a veil over her head and little muslin things over her hair, which was scraped back. She had a grey, cold face and her eyes were hollow and sunken. She was looking at me in a detached way, as if she were just looking at the spot where I was standing but couldn't see me as a person. I was scared but not terrified; an unseen presence is far more terrifying.

Room with a view and a visitor[†]

With so many hotels and boarding houses in the Malverns, it is only to be expected that at least one of them has a ghost. John Hobson owned a small hotel in West Malvern which has now been converted to other purposes.

As a family we had always had a desire to run an Hotel and in 1968 when our daughter had qualified in Hotel Management, we felt that the time was right to embark on this project. We therefore started to hunt for a suitable property (always remembering the limited funds at our disposal). We were living in Solihull at the time and spent many months scouring the West Midlands. It was a frustrating search, we investigated established hotels and large properties suitable for conversion, and there were always snags, either too large, not large enough, too expensive (the usual snag) and many other reasons not to buy.

We were really getting desperate when we came across what appeared to be 'just what we were looking for'. It was a medium-sized hotel, very old (part was well over 100 years old at the time) very run down and high up on the Malvern hills with wonderful views. It required a lot of renovation, decorating, etc (the main reason it fell within our budget).

It was run by an elderly couple, and in view of its age we queried as to whether it was haunted. They assured us that they had never been aware of any problems in this direction. As a family we had always been susceptible to atmospheres and we did not suspect anything untoward – how wrong we were proved to be.

Eventually, after another frustrating period of Bank Managers, Accountants, Estate Agents etc, we started on what proved to be an endless programme of decorating, plumbing, electrics, etc – you name it, we did it. We actually started with our first guests on the day we moved in, so you can imagine the utter chaos.

One night, chatting in the bar, one of the guests said, half-jokingly, 'In

[†]First submitted to BBC Hereford and Worcester for their ghost story competition.

the middle of last night our bedroom door opened and closed again'. We said, 'Pull the other' but he was adamant that it happened and that he had locked the door on retiring. (This was bedroom number 11 – remember this).

At about the same time we had two ladies (sisters) who looked after the bedrooms and they told us they did not like working on the top floor, especially in one bedroom, as they felt they were being watched. These ladies did not stay with us very long.

All went well until the following spring when one day, as we were sitting in our lounge (over which were empty bedrooms) we heard footsteps crossing the floor above. We went upstairs to investigate (knowing there was nobody in at the time) and what did we find? You have guessed it – nothing. This happened from time to time throughout the year, but more regularly every spring.

We had another lady who worked for us – a real treasure – who regularly lost her cleaning materials: polish, aerosols, etc. She would say 'I have lost such and such but I expect it will turn up'. And it always did, in some obscure place where she had never been.

I well remember one evening when we were chatting with some of the guests in the bar and the conversation turned to the question as to whether the place was haunted. One of the ladies said, 'There is nothing nasty here though' to which we replied 'What do you mean?' She said, 'Well, when we were here last year we were in the same room (this was number 11 – remember!) and during the night I heard footsteps coming down the corridor, presumably someone paying a visit to the toilet, but I never heard the toilet flush or the footsteps return. Then during last night, I heard the footsteps again, then, all at once, I saw a young boy standing in the corner of the bedroom, dressed in a Norfolk jacket, knee breeches and buckle shoes, with blonde hair cut in a shoulder-length bob. I was just about to say to him, 'What are doing here' when he vanished, and I am sure that whatever is here is friendly'.

Following this episode we made intensive enquiries into local history but could not find any reference to a young boy of this description. No doubt it happened too far back in the past for anyone to remember. For no particular reason we decided to call him Oliver, and from this time on all happenings were attributed to Oliver.

One of the most peculiar things that happened was the episode of the teapot. I will explain:

When we had guests to stay we always took a tray to their bedrooms with morning tea etc. It was my usual routine to collect these trays and, one such morning when the guests were down for breakfast, I collected all the trays and returned them to the kitchen to wash. Following my usual procedure, I cleared all the trays, put the cups and saucers in the dishwasher and lined all the teapots and jugs up on the kitchen table. Now, follow carefully:

I removed all the lids from the teapots and washed and dried them. I then washed all the teapots and jugs and as I dried each teapot I placed a lid on same, but when I had finished I had one teapot lid spare, with no teapot for it. Now!! You explain that?? We never found that teapot and the lid was on a shelf in the kitchen until we left.

We had a similar experience with the disappearance of a teacup from the dining room, but I will not worry you with the details.

Our stay at the hotel for ten years was a very happy one and our ghostly happenings were really only mischievous and never did anyone any harm. We hope that our successors have as much fun with Oliver as we had.

As I remarked in the title to this story, it really is true, and I have told it as it happened, so do sleep easily tonight.

Even more enchanting than the Malvern ghosts and legends is the music of Elgar. The Enigma Variations, Dream of Gerontius and Pomp and Circumstances were all composed as he walked the Malvern hills. He was born in Worcester in 1857 but the town was slow to recognise his genius. He scraped a living as a private music teacher and when he married one of his pupils her family disowned them both. Now there are many who cannot walk the Malvern hills without the haunting strains of his music coming to mind.

CLENT AND THE LICKEYS

 OME TWO HUNDRED MILLION YEARS AGO, when prehistoric monsters roamed the land, a huge rush of salt water swept across what is now the Midland Plain, dumping great heaps of coarse fragments from cliffs and mountainsides at its south-western edge. This debris became the Clent and Lickey Hills, which stretch for eleven miles and include the highest summit in the central Midlands, Walton Hill at Clent. Although the suburbs have crept to their feet the hills themselves remain as beautiful as ever, with peaks rising from natural woodland filled with birds and flowers. The gentle slopes of the northern edge are an appropriate setting for the story of the martyrdom of Saint Kenelm.

The legend of King Kenelm

Barrie Roberts

When Kenulf, King of Mercia died in 819, he left one young son, Kenelm, and two daughters, of whom Quendrada was the eldest. Quendrada conspired with her lover to murder Kenelm and take over the kingdom. Out riding with Kenelm in the Cowbach valley, between Clent and Romsley, the lover slew the young king, cut off his head and hid the body under a thornbush.

Months later, as the Pope officiated at Saint Peter's in Rome, a snow-white dove flew in through a window and dropped a scroll from its beak. On the scroll was a message which read:

> *In Clent, in Cowbach, lyeth under a thorn*
> *His head off-shorn, Kenelm, King born.*

Intrigued, the Pope sent messengers to England to investigate. Looking for a buried body in the wild and desolate countryside was like looking for a needle in a haystack but the searchers were guided to the spot by a shaft of light and the lowing of a milk white cow. As they disinterred the corpse, a spring gushed from the ground.

Divine vengeance had not done with Quendrada, however. Giraldus Cambrensis, in *The Journey through Wales* (1188, translated L Thorpe Penguin 1978) tells of another miracle that struck the guilty queen:

When the body of Kenelm was carried out and the crowd shouted: 'He is God's martyr! There is no doubt about it! He is the martyr of God!' Quendrada, who was guilty of her brother's murder and had it very much on her conscience, replied:'He is indeed God's martyr, as truly as my eyes are resting on this Psalter!'. By chance, she was reading the Psalter at the moment. Thereupon, by divine intervention, her two eyes were torn from her head and fell plop on the open book, where you can still see the marks of her blood to this day.

She died not long afterwards, and her body was left to rot in an open ditch.

You cannot now see the bloodstained Psalter. It used to be a prized possession of Winchcombe Abbey, where, Giraldus tells us, it once clung to the hands of an impious monk who had had intercourse with a woman in the Abbey precincts during the vigil of Saint Kenelm, and later had the audacity to carry the Psalter in the procession relics. It refused to let go of him until he confessed.

You can see Saint Kenelm's spring, carefully protected, next to Saint Kenelm's Church, just over a mile north west of Romsley, and while you are there, have a look at the 750 year-old carving over the Church door.

St. Kenelm's Church, Clent.

Nowadays concealed corpses are sought with sniffer dogs, heat seeking cameras and soil-resistivity instruments, but when these fail there are still occasions when the mysterious abilities of psychics, like the Dutchman Gerard Croiset, seem able to locate bodies. Is the story of Kenelm, a version of such an incident, distorted by a thousand years of re-telling and belief in miracles?

He forgot his head

Those who walk their dogs through the woods of the Lickey Hills may be surprised to know that when the Worcester–Birmingham road was turnpiked in
1726, the hills were a desolate moorland with few trees. It was a lonely and dangerous spot, a favourite haunt of highwaymen who would jump out as the horses
were tiring and slowing down after the long pull up the Lickey incline. The last
two Lickey Highwaymen, Brady and Johnson, were hanged at Worcester in 1806.
A curious legend exists concerning Brady which is included in this story, told
by an Engineer living on the Bromsgrove side of the Lickey Hills.

Strange things go on in the Lickeys near the time of the summer solstice.
I often walk with the dogs round the western side of the hills into the pine
woods off Monument Lane. I can go there one evening when I can see that
the ground is covered by pine needles and cones, then early the next
morning I find that the ground beneath four or five trees has been cleared
in a large circle and the wild flowers are pushed up into the bark of the pine
trees to make a pattern. I've asked the locals and they say it must be part
of the solstice when all kinds of weird people come out to the hills but
the strange thing is, in all the twenty years I've lived here, I've never seen
anyone actually doing anything.

My home is not far from Monument Lane and we hadn't been here
for long before locals started to tell us strange stories, one of which referred
to a horse with a headless rider. In the mid-summer of 1979, my wife and
I had retired to bed quite early while it was still light and were just going
off to sleep when we heard a clippety-clop at the side of our bungalow.
We looked at each other and said, 'Could this be right?' To get on to the
path at the side of our house you would need to go through a thick hedge.
With that, I got out of bed and very bravely (but accompanied by the dogs)
went to see what was happening. I was just in time to see the rear view of
a headless guy mounted on a horse going away from me down the path
by the side of our home.

I don't know much about horses but I can tell you that this was a chest-
nut horse. The man astride it had riding boots and was wearing a grey
frock-type coat which parted so that it could flow either side of the saddle.
He was holding his reins in his right hand with his head under his left arm.
He was quite solid and looked very real except for his misplaced head. I
only saw him for a few seconds before he turned right and went through
the gap in my hedge out of sight.

It occurred to me afterwards that someone could have been playing a prank but if so, it was exceptionally well done, also I have had a word with one or two families I thought capable of perpetrating such a prank and they have assured me that they haven't done anything.

Being an engineer by profession, I believe that everything has to have a reason so I have put forward my story over many a gin and tonic. It would appear that, before it was abolished in 1868, a gibbet stood on the old Birmingham Road just by the Lickey Church. At the back end of the 1700's a guy who was reputed to have had the name of Brady got into trouble with the law. He was tried and found guilty but before he was suspended from the gibbet his head got separated from his body so that they had some difficulty stringing the torso up. It is said that this guy returns to get his revenge on the people of the Lickeys for the atrocities that had befallen his body.

Brady would have been hung at Worcester, then once the public hanging was over his body would probably have been brought back to a local gibbet (no-one is certain exactly where the gibbet stood) and hung from there. Perhaps Brady had been accidentally decapitated at Worcester. Incidentally the crossbeam from the gibbet is said to have been used as a hearth beam in one of the nineteenth century cottages in Warren Lane nearby.

BIBLIOGRAPHY

In addition to local guides and reference books, the following have been especially useful:

* *The Victoria County History, A History of the County of Worcestershire,* published for The University of London Institute of Historical Research, 1913.

* *The Worcestershire Village Book,* reprinted 1992, published jointly by Countryside Books, Newbury and the WFWI, Worcester.

* Allies Jabez, *Antiquities and Folk-lore of Worcestershire,* Parker and Grainger, 1856.

* Avery William, *The William Avery Memorial Volumes,* Volume 1, collated cuttings from Redditch Indicator and other local newspapers, 1823 – 1899, (in Redditch library).

* Bradford Anne, Roberts Barrie and Roberts John, *Midland Ghosts and Hauntings,* Quercus 1994.

* Drewitt John and Roberts John, *Midland Rivers & Streams,* Quercus, 1995.

* Gwillam Bill, *Old Worcester, People and Places,* published by Rose Hill Teacher's Centre, 1977.

* Peacock John, *Costume 1066 – 1996,* reprinted Thames and Hudson 1992.

* Pevsner Nikolaus, *Worcestershire,* from the Buildings of England series, reprinted 1985, Penguin.

* Skipp Victor, *The Centre of England,* Eyre Methuen, London, 1979.

* Willis Bund JW, *The Civil War in Worcestershire, 1642 – 1646,* published by Alan Sutton Publishing Ltd, 1979.

* Woodward J, *The History of Bordesley Abbey,* Publisher unknown, 1866.

Some of the information on medieval history has been obtained from relevant weekend courses at The Hill Residential College, Abergavenny.